VENUS OBSERVED

A revival of the play was staged at the Chichester Festival Theatre in 1992, with the following cast of characters:

Duke of Altair	Donald Sinden
Edgar	Jeremy Brudnell
Reedbeck	Denis Quilley
Dominic	Robert Portall
Rosabel Fleming	Kate O'Mara
Jessie Dill	Jean Boht
Reddleman	Michael G Jones
Bates	Roy Holder
Hilda	Alexandra Bastedo
Perpetua	Susannah Harker

The play was directed by James Roose-Evans
Designed by Poppy Mitchell

SYNOPSIS OF SCENES

ACT I
SCENE 1 The Observatory Room at Stellmere Park, the Duke's mansion. A morning in Autumn
SCENE 2 The Temple of the Ancient Virtues, Stellmere Park. That afternoon

ACT II
SCENE 1 The Observatory Room. That night
SCENE 2 The Temple of the Ancient Virtues. Later that night

VENUS OBSERVED

First produced by Sir Laurence Olivier at the St James's Theatre, London, on 18th January, 1950, with the following cast:

Hereward, the Duke of Altair	Laurence Olivier
Edgar, his son, the Marquis of Charlock	Denholm Elliott
Herbert Reedbeck, his Estate Manager	George Relph
Dominic, his son	Robert Beaumont
Rosabel Fleming	Valerie Taylor
Jessie Dill	Brenda de Banzie
Captain Fox Reddleman, butler	Fred Johnson
Bates, footman	Thomas Heathcote
Hilda Taylor-Snell	Rachel Kempson
Perpetua, Reedbeck's daughter	Heather Stannard

Design by Roger Furse

ACT I

Scene 1

The Observatory Room at Stellmere Park. A morning in Autumn

A room at the top of a mansion: once a bedroom, now an observatory

When the CURTAIN rises the Duke of Altair is in argument with his son Edgar. Also present is Herbert Reedbeck, the Duke's agent

Duke Anyone would think I had made some extraordinary
Suggestion. But in fact how natural it is.
Aren't you my son?

Edgar Yes, Father, of course I am.

Duke Then it's up to you to choose who shall be your mother.
Does that seem to you improper, Reedbeck?

Reedbeck No,
Your Grace; it's not, perhaps, always done,
But few parents consider their children as you do.
I don't dislike the plan at all.

Edgar I sweat
With embarrassment.

Duke You have been
Too much with the horses. This, that I ask you to do,
Is an act of poetry, and a compliment
To the freshness of your mind. Why should you sweat?
Here they will be, three handsome women,
All of them at some time implicated
In the joyous routine of my life. (I could scarcely
Put it more delicately.) I wish to marry.
Who am I, in heaven's name, to decide
Which were my vintage years of love?
Good God, to differentiate between
The first bright blow on my sleeping flesh,
The big breasts of mid-morning,
And the high old dance of afternoon—
Value one against the other? Never, not I,

Till the eschatological rain shall lay my dust.
But you, dear boy, with your twenty-five impartial years,
Can perform the judgement of Paris,
Can savour, consider, and award the apple
With a cool hand. You will find an apple
Over there by the spectroscope.

Edgar   But why must you marry?
Or, if that's an impertinence, why do I have to have
A mother? I've been able to grow to a sizable boy
Without one.

Duke   Why? Because I see no end
To the parcelling out of heaven in small beauties,
Year after year, flocks of girls, who look
So lately kissed by God
They come out on the world with lips shining,
Flocks and generations, until time
Seems like nothing so much
As a blinding snowstorm of virginity,
And a man, lost in the perpetual scurry of white,
Can only close his eyes
In a resignation of monogamy.

Edgar Anyway, it would be impossibly hasty
Judgement. Honour you as I may, I don't
See how I can do it.

Duke   If Paris had no trouble
Choosing between the tide-turning beauty,
Imponderable and sexed with eternity,
Of Aphrodite, Hera and Athene,
Aren't you ashamed to make heavy weather of a choice
Between Hilda, and Rosabel, and Jessie?
And if you can't make up your mind about a woman
At first meeting, all hope of definition has gone;
Prejudice, delirium, or rage
Will cock their snooks, and the apple will go bad.
No, boy, no; go and water your horses
And come back and choose your mother.

Edgar   At what time?

Duke What is it now?

Reedbeck   Five past eleven.

Duke   They should
Be here. At eleven twenty-nine we're to have

The total eclipse of the sun, to which I've invited them.
The mouth of the moon has already begun to munch.
We shall all feel ourselves making a north-west passage
Through the sea of heaven, and darkness will cover
The face of the earth. In that moment
All women will be as one.

Edgar   That's what I was going
To ask you. I don't want to play the heavy son,
But would you say you loved these women equally?

Duke Equality is a mortuary word. Just choose.
Shall I be happy on Tuesdays, Thursdays, and Saturdays.
Or on Mondays, Wednesdays, and Fridays? Some such difference
Is all that your choice involves.

Captain Fox Reddleman, a manservant, enters. He looks like, and was once, a lion tamer

Reddleman   'Scuse, your Grace:
But a telegram for our little friend Mr Reedbeck.
A telegram, Mr Reedbeck. B'Jason, four
Flights I've had to come up to bring it to you.
Please Jenny it's worth it. And the boy's waiting.

Edgar Well, Father, I don't know; with a certain sense
Of preconceiving myself, I may come back.
I shall do what I can for you; I only hope
You'll not live to regret the way my fancy
Takes you.

Edgar exits

Reedbeck Oh! Would you ever think
Such a joy could happen to me, in the world as we know it?

Reddleman I have to tell your Grace, in all decency
To the footman Bates, who I religiously despise,
If the fellow comes on duty with a bloody nose
'Tis my doing, and long may it bleed. And h'wot
About the boy below, Mr Reedbeck? Any answer?

Reedbeck No, no, Reddleman, only thanksgiving.
Oh, and I suppose a shilling, he'd like a shilling.

Duke And go gently with Bates, Reddleman, or else
You'll drive him back to his old nervous habits
Of biting his nails and burglary. Remember
You're not a lion tamer now.

Reddleman   And that
  Was a hit below—I'm wearing no belt—below
  The navel. Thank God I'm severed from my mother
  Or she would have felt it severely. I'd remind you
  'Twas fighting for king and country I lost me nerve.
  And b'Daniel, it's a sad job to be parted
  From the lords of the jungle.

Duke   I'm sorry, Reddleman;
  I wasn't meaning to hurt you.

Reddleman   Well, go easy,
  Go easy with me, your Grace. Now, Mr Reedbeck:
  Thanksgiving and a bob for the boy below:
  Very good.

  Reddleman exits

Reedbeck A red-letter day for me, your Grace;
  Let me see: the twenty-ninth of October?

Duke   Yes;
  The leaves transfigured by the thought of death,
  The wind south-west, a blue sky buffaloed
  By cloud, the sun approaching its eclipse.

Reedbeck You remember I have a daughter? I've spoken of her
  From time to time; I had the astounding fortune
  To beget her, as though I'd been chosen to release
  A rose from the world's rock; and then I had
  The misery to lose her, when her mother
  Left me for America, ten years ago.
  Well, now I'm holding in my hand a message
  Which says she's returning to me, returning to-day,
  No time of arrival, just bare and astonishing
  "Am in England hope to kiss you before lunch
  Perpetua." I can hardly believe it could happen,
  I can't believe so, not in the world as we know it.

Duke Go easy, Reedbeck, go easy with yourself.

Reedbeck If she should come in time for the eclipse——

Duke Then, of course, she shall join us to see the eclipse.
  It will be a change for her after America.
  I'm going now, to dress. Subdue yourself, Reedbeck.
  Otherwise you'll capsize in disappointment.
  Expect the worst.

The Duke exits

Reedbeck   Not at all, oh, not at all,
No shadows of that sort.

(*He goes to the telephone, dials and hums into the receiver*)

                                 Must warn my housekeeper.
"I galloped, Dirck galloped, we galloped all three ..."
Oh, Mrs Lendy, Mr Reedbeck here; I have to ask you
To prepare a room for my daughter. I'm so glad
To hear you gasp. However, we must keep our heads,
Such as they are. Tell her to join us here
And ask to be shown to the Observatory Room.
There will be refreshment for her, and a total
Eclipse of the sun.

Dominic, Reedbeck's son, enters

Dominic   I want to speak to you.
How long are we likely to be alone?

Reedbeck   In a moment,
Dominic dear. You'll put her some flowers, Mrs Lendy.
Are the Helianthus gone? Well, *uliginosum*.
You call them chrysanthemums, I think. And on her bed
The lilac linen sheets. Some time before lunch.
Good-bye. Oh, Dominic, my dear, dear boy,
Your sister's coming home!

Dominic (*silent, and then*)   That makes you happy.

Reedbeck Oh, dear, it's one of your knock-the-bottom-
Out-of-everything mornings. Or do you mean
You've heard, and you know what's bringing her home?
I hope nothing's amiss?

Dominic   Not with her.

Reedbeck   Well, then—

Dominic Do I say what I have to say *here*? Or do we go back
To the house? It isn't going to be pleasant.

Reedbeck   Of course it is.
There's nothing unpleasant that isn't going to be pleasant.
Perpetua's returning to me; the world

Is no longer depressed at the poles, and everything
Will be pleasant: the east wind, smoking fires,
Revolution, debility—

Dominic   Jail?

Reedbeck   Yes, jail.
Solitary confinement, the cat-o'-nine-tails,
Your Aunt Florence—

Dominic   Can you keep your feet
On sober earth for five difficult minutes
And talk responsibly? Why are we so rich?
I've asked you before; but you, a Duke's bailiff,
An agent: where did our money come from?

Reedbeck Have you no capacity for delight?
Do for all our sakes be pleasant, dear boy.

Dominic You said our money came from legacies, you told me
From legacies!

Reedbeck   Just so; we've been very fortunate.
Your uncle Hector, when he put on immortality
In Tasmania, increased, to a certain extent,
Our freedom from care; and old Lady Bright, my first
Employer, when she passed on, passed on
Herself to heaven and the rest to me; and then—

Dominic I have to ask for figures. My Uncle Hector
Died leaving—?

Reedbeck   Don't let's talk of death.
I've a heart this morning as light as a nebula.
But you, you sombre boy, you can't even
Sputter up a few sparks when I tell you
Your sister's coming home!

Dominic   Died, leaving—?

Reedbeck   Really,
How can I be expected to remember?
There was some music, certainly; the piano score
Of *The Quaker Girl*; and I recollect some ninepins;
And a small South American lizard called Faithful
Which died in quarantine. But Lady Bright—

Act I, Scene 1

Dominic You've stolen the money, haven't you: steadily
And consistently? O God, why ask? I know
Already. And thieved with so little subtlety
Anyone might know. Raised rents
But entered in your books at the old figure;
Sale of produce and timber, at prices higher
Than you've recorded. I've been ferreting,
Ever since an unmistakable innuendo
From Bates the footman.

Reedbeck   Come now; Bates
Is a common burglar, and sees, of course,
His reflection in all about him. He was caught
Red-handed with the silver, and his Grace,
Being short of staff at the time, asked him to stay
And clean it.

Dominic   Bates is quite a decent fellow.
I've had a long talk to him. He used to suffer
From a pathological lust for climbing ladders
And had to rationalize it when he got
To the top. And now he's determined to be honest,
Even if it makes him ill, he says. But with you
It's unrelieved, wicked cupidity.
Of course I go down from Cambridge. I couldn't stay there
When any morning I might wake up and find
I'd become the son of a convict. We're both in
For misery now, and Perpetua comes home
Just in time to share it.

Reedbeck   I wish I could explain
How very mistaken I'm sure you must be. Especially
On such a cheerful morning. It's really too bad.
We have the dark every twelve hours as it is
Without inventing more.

*Bates enters. He shows a trace of rough handling. He announces Miss
Rosabel Fleming, and withdraws*

Rosabel Fleming enters

Rosabel   Oh, I am sorry.
Perhaps I am here too soon. I thought—

Reedbeck   The competitors!
I'd forgotten them. Forgive me, dear lady.
You find me a little put about.

Rosabel   I thought the Duke—

Reedbeck You are perfectly right. His Grace will join us shortly.
　You are perfectly right. I am Harold Reedbeck,
　The estate manager. This was my son.

Rosabel How do you do? But—*was* your son?

Reedbeck There's no tense for me now except the past,
　Miss Hemming. You were Miss Hemming?

Rosabel   Fleming
　At almost any time I am Rosabel Fleming.

Dominic Please excuse me. I'd like to know you, of course,
　But I can't look anyone happily in the eye.
　I am pleased to have met you.

　Dominic exits

Rosabel   Is he in some trouble?

Reedbeck The paradoxes of virtue have confused him.
　But do please, sit down.

Rosabel   I begin to see
　Why the theatre gives me so little work.
　That could scarcely have been called a splendid entrance,
　Even by the most loving.

Reedbeck   Go down from Cambridge.
　Did you hear him say that? No, you were not here.
　It let all the life out of me for a moment.

Rosabel I think we're both of us feeling disturbed, Mr Reedbeck.
　We must try to put ourselves in order again.

Reedbeck All the Latin I have myself, you know,
　Is purely botanical: *muscari cosmosum monstrosum*
　And *scrophularia nodosa*—that kind of thing.
　But how I longed as a boy
　For the groves and grooves of Academe.
　Give me civilization, Miss Fleming;
　You can keep your progress.

Rosabel   It's rather disconcerting
　To have been shown so mysteriously up to this room.
　What is happening?

Reedbeck   Ah, the Observatory Room—
It gives, you see, onto an uninterrupted
Sweep of the Surrey heavens, and at night
Our rich inheritance—

Rosabel   You mean—

Reedbeck   The stars,
Miss Fleming, the glorious universe.

Mrs Jessie Dill enters

Jessie Oh, pardon me. Have I gone wrong? I asked
Where the Duke would be.

Reedbeck   Quite so, and, yes,
His Grace should be here. Indeed he should be.
And why ever didn't Bates—

Jessie   I'm Mrs Dill.
It's my own fault the man hasn't announced me.
It seemed to me "All those stairs for the poor chap
Just to say Here's Jessie". He went on insisting,
Of course, but when we got to the second landing
He must have thought it was getting undignified
Both of us coming up two steps at a time.
So he slid back down the banisters.
                    (*To Rosabel*)   I can't
Help feeling we've met before. I know your face
So very well.

Rosabel   My name's Rosabel Fleming.

Jessie Well, that's it, of course. I should have remembered.
I saw you once, it must be years ago now,
Being very sweet in a play about Ophelia.
And this is a strange thing, too, being up here
In this room together. You'd hardly recognize it.
Well, I don't know, I should say that's a telescope.

Reedbeck We were talking about this room when you came, Mrs Dill.
My name is Reedbeck. This was one of His Grace's
Bedrooms, as perhaps ... But now, as you see,
He prefers to regard the skies here,
Combing through the night for knowledge. He also uses
The room for experiments.

Jessie   He always did.

Rosabel Please, Mr Reedbeck, if you would give the Duke
My apologies, I won't stay now.
Will you tell him that, finding myself not far away,
I simply looked in for a moment—

The Duke enters

Duke   Good morning, Rosabel.
Good morning Jessie.
Have you made yourself known to each other?

Jessie Here he is, God bless him, not looking a day older,
Even if he does have to use a telescope.

Duke Flattery, Jessie; for years the frost has lain
On my stubble beard. The swallows and other such
Migratory birds have left me months ago.
And I must ask you both to forgive me for keeping you waiting.
I was up all night with the universe again
And slept late. Is that not to be forgiven?
A silence broods on Rosabel.

Rosabel   Yes, I know,
I'm very conscious of it. I may be dreaming—
The old dream of being out there on the stage
With no idea what part I was playing. I don't
Really know why I am here.

Duke   Why, Rosabel,
For a total eclipse of the sun.
Didn't I mention it to you in my letter?

Rosabel Is it a family custom to disinter
Old friendships during an eclipse?
Or what other reason? It's not your birthday?
No, you're Sagittarian. This is only October.

Duke And the leaves are falling. What shall a robin do then,
Poor thing?

Jessie   Sit in this barn and keep himself warm
Tucked up alone in the west wing, poor thing.

Edgar, the Duke's son, enters

Duke My son Edgar, Miss Rosabel Fleming.

I introduce Rosabel first, Jessie, to give you
Time to enjoy your joke. My son Edgar,
Mrs Dill.

Jessie   How lovely to meet you, Edgar.
I've known your father, you know, why, ever since
I was ever so slim. In the days when my husband
Was a friend of your father's.
I hope he'll allow me to say his friend.

Duke   Of course,
Of course. How well did I know him?

Edgar   It's just as well
We understand my father.

Rosabel   God knows, it's not easy.
Like having to depend on a tourist's phrase book
In a foreign city. How to make human sense
Out of words that don't care if they're comprehensible
To the heart that hears them.

Duke We're not, I hope, in this mellow October light
Getting ill at ease? We're here this morning to watch
The sun annulled and renewed, and to sit affectionately
Over the year's dilapidation. "Mellow"
Is the keynote of the hour. We must be mellow,
Remembering we've been on the earth two million years,
Man and boy and Sterkfontein ape.

Reedbeck (*singing abstractedly at the window*)
You call me old
But I am still
A chippy young chap on Chipperton Hill
And shall be, while
My flesh can cover
The bones of a bona-fide lover.
Heydilly, heydilly, hang me a sheep.

Duke Happy, happy Reedbeck. He has a daughter
Returning to him.

Jessie   And there he sits and purrs
As though the morning was a saucer of milk.

Reedbeck I caught myself singing. I do beg your pardon.

Edgar Sing away, Reedbeck. Bring her in with music.
This is wonderful news.

Bates appears at the door to announce Mrs Hilda Taylor-Snell

Reedbeck Can this be—is it . . . ?

Mrs Hilda Taylor-Snell enters

Duke The exact Hilda. Punctuality
Was drawing its last breath. The sun has mooned
Away half its light already.

Hilda   A party, Hereward?
You didn't tell me.

Duke   I scarcely knew. And anyway
We shall all feel quite alone, except, perhaps, Jessie.
Mrs Dill, Mrs Taylor-Snell. There will only be
The appearance of people being near to us.
Miss Rosabel Fleming, Mrs Taylor-Snell.
Reedbeck you know. You've disappointed him.
He hoped you would have been his daughter.

Hilda Did you ever propose it, Reedbeck?

Reedbeck   You see before you
A creaking bough on which, at any moment,
A dear young daughter may alight.

Duke My extension in time: Edgar.

Edgar   Five feet ten
Of my unlimited father.

Hilda   I have often
Expected to meet you.

Edgar   I suppose so;
But until he's dead I'm really a redundancy.
I make him feel bifurcated.

Jessie   Wherever
Does he learn those terrible words?

Edgar   I spend
Such a lot of my time in the stables.

Bates is loitering by the door

Duke (*to Bates*) What is it, Bates?

Bates   There are faces
  As can be mauled about wiv, and there are faces
  As can't be mauled about wiv. Mine can't
  Be mauled about wiv. Memo, guvnor, to be 'anded
  On to the proper quarters, and *you* know
  What basket I refers to.
  Will that be all, guvnor?

Duke   That will be all, Bates.

  Bates exits

Reedbeck throws open the window and leans out

Hilda Be careful, Reedbeck! There really is such a thing
  As the force of gravity.

Reedbeck   Only the wind blowing
  And the rattle of leaves. I hoped it would prove to be
  Internal combustion.

Duke (*aside to Edgar*) I should have mentioned to you,
  The case of Athene is minutely complicated
  By a husband. But don't be deflected. He would still
  Have the shooting over the estate. Nothing
  Is insurmountable.

Edgar   Except yourself,
  I take you to mean. But it's all right;
  I'm devoted to you.

Hilda   Why don't you give it up,
  Reedbeck? There's no daughter there. How much
  This house has aged, Hereward, since I saw it
  Last. I was thinking so coming up the stairs.
  It looks as though the walls have cried themselves
  To sleep for nights on end. And the number of windows
  Broken! I don't think you should throw nearly
  So many stones. The spiders are larger, the jackdaws
  Ruder, the servants more eccentric. You mustn't
  Drift into Gothic, when your physique is so
  Stubbornly Norman.

Duke   I see no point in trying
To make time look as though it were standing still
By renewing the face of it. I like to watch my own
Deft and reckless plunge into ancient history.
It assuages my lust for speed. Dark glasses for the ladies,
Reedbeck; tell them to look at the sun.

Edgar   And to pray
For all small birds under the eye of the hawk.

Jessie I can remember, when I was a kid,
Being got out of bed and told I had to look
At something in the sky. I kept saying
Oh, yes, mum, isn't it lovely, isn't it lovely?
It was a comet or a zeppelin or something.
But all I could see was the usual end
Of the Crystal Palace.

Reedbeck (*handing Jessie dark glasses*) Look at the sun, Mrs Dill.

Jessie And now I can't help feeling
As if I'd just been got out of bed again
To look at something I probably shan't see.

Duke That's the human predicament, in a nutshell.

Rosabel There's a kind of humour abroad this morning that seems to
Put me outside the party.

Reedbeck   Look at the sun, Miss Fleming.

Rosabel Thank you.

Edgar   I've such a feeling of pre-natal
Tension, it's more than a boy can bear. Father,
I'm going to make the decision now
And pin the future down for you.

Hilda   But will you
Find that easy? I couldn't help overhearing.
The future has the most uncertain temper.
After all you've said, Hereward, do you teach
Your child to tamper with time?

Duke   He had it to play with
When he was young; but he'll soon see
How it will rag him to death. Meanwhile, the eclipse.
Let me be your guide. Observe how Sol Salome

Almost hidden by the head of the Baptist moon
Dances her last few steps of fire.

Hilda   You're confusing
The sex of the sun.

Duke   It's the act itself; observe
The copulation of Jove, magnificent in
Mid air.

Jessie   The bulk of the moon, creeping on
And on. It makes me feel more solemn than I've ever
Felt before at eleven o'clock in the morning.

Edgar No nice eclipse for you, Miss Fleming?

Rosabel   Why yes,
It was what your father invited me to see.
I was far away for the moment.

Edgar   Before you go
To the window, I wonder if you'd mind accepting this apple?

Rosabel No, thank you. I'll go and see what there is to be seen
Before it's too late.

Edgar   Father, may I have your attention?
There, Miss Fleming, it will come in useful sometime.

Duke Daylight, you see, is shamming twilight. Nature
Is being made a fool of. Three or four stars, there,
You can see them wince, where only a moment earlier
Morning was all serene. The crows, with much
Misgiving, talk themselves into their trees. Even
The usually phlegmatic owls
Care a hoot or two. The bats from the barn
Make one flickering flight, and return to hang
Their heads. All of them tricked and fuddled
By the passing of a small cadaverous planet.

Hilda Yes, we understand the event perfectly.

Jessie Let him enjoy it. Space, ever and ever,
On and on ... Well, I don't know.

Edgar Father, I don't know whether you have noticed;
A certain event has occurred.

Duke   Is now occurring.
We're crossing perceptibly into the dark.
Daylight differences are made subordinate
To the general shade.

Edgar   Father, for God's sake, look!
I am giving Miss Fleming an apple.

Rosabel   You've already
Given me an apple.

Duke   I observe you're plying
Rosabel with fruit. *Bis dat qui cito dat.*
We can now turn our attention again to the sun.

Edgar So a revolutionary change begins
Without raising a hand's turn of the dust.
Ah, well; give me some dark glass.

Hilda   What a shame
If that cloud spoils the climax for us.

Reedbeck   No.
It avoids, you see; it glides mercifully
And dexterously past. I hope and pray
The same will be true of the cloud that hangs over my own
Sunshine: but young men can be so ruthless,
So ruthless; it's terrible to think about.

Duke What now, Reedbeck?

Reedbeck   Ah, yes; to the cosmos it doesn't
Matter; I suppose I agree.

Jessie   To think
We're in the shadow of old Lunabella.

Duke   To think.

Jessie When she moves over will she see us
Coming out of her shadow? Are we really
As bright as a moon, from the moon's side of the question?

Duke We have a borrowed brilliance. At night
Among the knots and clusters and corner boys
Of the sky, among asteroids and cepheids,
With Sirius, Mercury, and Canis Major,
Among nebulae and magellanic cloud,
You shine, Jessie.

Jessie   You're making me self-conscious.

Duke Here, we're as dull as unwashed plates; out there
We shine. That's a consideration. Come
Close to paradise, and where's the lustre?
But still, at some remove, we shine, and truth
We hope is content to keep a distant prospect.
So you, Jessie, and the swamps of the equator,
Shine; the boring overplus of ocean,
The Walworth Road, the Parthenon, and Reedbeck
Shine; the dark trees with the nightingale
At heart, dockyards, the desert, the newly dead,
Minarets, gasometers, and even I
Fall into space in one not unattractive
Beam. To take us separately is to stare
At mud; only together, at long range,
We coalesce in light.

Jessie   I like to think I'm being
A ray of light to some nice young couple out there;
"There's the Great Bear," they'd say, and "Look,
There's old Jessie, tilted on her side
Just over the Charing Cross Hotel."

Hilda   You both
Chatter so. It's a moment for quiet. Who knows
If ever I'll see this again.

Edgar   The end of our lord
The sun.

Rosabel   It's no good. I must get out into the air!
It's impossible to breathe up here!

Duke   What is it,
Rosabel? Claustrophobia on the brink
Of the free heavens? Come now, think of it
As the usual dipping of day's flag. You used
To love this room at night.

Rosabel   How do you know?
How do you know what I or anyone else
Has ever felt, let alone ever loved.
You without a beat of heart worth measuring?
You sit up here all night looking at the stars,
Travelling farther and farther away from living people.
I hate your telescope!
You would never believe there are some affections
Which would rather have decent burial

Than this mocking reinstatement you offer them.
You're a devil, a devil, a devil!

Duke   Only
On one side of the family, Rosabel,
Please believe that.

Edgar (*taking the apple from her hand*)
                         I beg your pardon; I think
I've made a mistake.

Rosabel   Oh, God, why can't I grow up
And learn to behave as though nothing mattered
Except to learn the lines of the part as they're written,
For the play's sake. I am very sorry.
It's very stupid of me to have spoilt the eclipse.

Duke It's frankly impossible to spoil the eclipse.

Reedbeck It would be fanciful no doubt to say
That the moon has placed a penny not
On the dead but on the living eye of the sun.

Edgar Yes, Reedbeck, it would.

Jessie   Don't you be put down.
It's nice that anyone can say anything at all.

Duke So Rosabel believes when the cold spell comes
And we're compelled to enter this draughty time
And shuffle about in the slipshod leaves,
Leaves disbanded, leaves at a loose end,
And we know we're in for the drifting of the fall,
We should merely shiver and be silent: never speak
Of the climate of Eden, or the really magnificent
Foliage of the tree of knowledge,
Or the unforgettable hushed emerald
Of the coiling and fettering serpent:
Pretend we never knew it, because love
Quite naturally condescended
To the passing of time. But why should we, Rosabel?

Hilda But if what I gather to be true is true,
Though it's no business of mine,
I must say, Hereward, you certainly seem to have been
Coruscating on thin ice. I think
She has cause to be angry. I do think so.
You've behaved a great deal less than well.

Duke I've behaved according to my lights of love
  Which were excellent and bright and much to be
  Remembered. You have all of you been my moments
  Of revelation. I wish I understood why
  You want to behave like skeletons in my cupboard.

Jessie Not Jessie, alas; her weight is all against it.
  But need we make Miss Fleming cry?

Edgar   I'd like it,
  Father, if Mrs Dill would have this apple.

Jessie I'd like it, too; though it's prettier on the tree.

Rosabel Moments of revelation! I only wonder what we revealed.
  Certainly not what goes on in other hearts than your own.
  That's as remote to you as a seaside lodging-house
  To a passing whale.

Hilda   Could she put it more fairly?

Jessie I remember seeing what was thought to be a whale
  At somewhere like Tenby; at least, my Father said
  Look, there's a whale, Jessie; but all I saw
  Was the tip of a fin which might have been
  Father Neptune or an old forgotten Channel swimmer.

Duke Rosabel—

Jessie We might as well never have changed the subject.

Duke Rosabel, why pick on me to be
  The villain? I'm a Roman in a world
  Of Romans, and all creation can recognize me
  As genus Man. Old men, young men, virgins,
  Viragoes, all walk hand in hand with me
  In the green enclosure of insensibility.
  An individual torment in Indo-China
  Makes less noise in your ear than the drop of a fir cone.
  So why do I have to be sensible
  Of a heart which is fortunate enough to be
  Four thousand miles nearer my way, someone,
  Moreover, to whom I've already given pleasure
  And the refuge of a bed, which I never gave
  (Such is my frailty) to the Indo-Chinee?
  Don't let's go mad with inconsistency.
  Either everything shall be near, or everything
  Shall be far. Allow me the wrong end of the telescope;
  I like to conform.

Now then, Mr Reedbeck,
u propose the vote of thanks to the speaker.

Reedbeck I've been listening, you know, for the sound of a taxi—
I've heard it, I think, just a few moments ago.

Rosabel Oh, mercy, what's the good of apologizing
And then going on just as I did before?
I'll go now, and leave some peace behind me.
(*She feels in her handbag and with a
smile plays a mock Ophelia*)
"My lord, I have remembrances of yours,
That I have longed long to re-deliver.
I pray you now receive them."

Duke   Rosabel—

Rosabel (*putting a packet of letters on the table*) There, my lord.

Duke Rosabel, this isn't a part I remember.

Rosabel It'll come to you. I'll say goodbye, then.

Duke I shall plough up the orchard, Edgar;
It was never a great success.

*As Rosabel moves towards the door the shadow lifts from the sun, and the light
falls on:*

Perpetua Reedbeck, wearing slacks, a bag slung over her shoulder

Edgar   God be praised,
The sun again!

Reedbeck   My daughter, it's my daughter,
Perpetua, my dear!

Perpetua runs to Reedbeck

Rosabel (*trying to laugh, but tears take over*)
"And I of ladies
Most deject and wretched! Woe is me!"

Rosabel exits

Reedbeck O my little sixpenny ha'penny daughter,
Home again, home again!

Hilda (*thinking of Rosabel*) I think, Hereward,
She could do with some company, that woman,
I'll ask her.

Hilda follows Rosabel

Perpetua Let me look at you. Every feature where I left it
Ten years ago! I'd forgotten you were so beautiful.

Reedbeck You mustn't spoil me, not so soon;
I shall puff myself up and explode like a frog.

Perpetua Perhaps we should sing until we're used to it?
Might that be the wise thing?

Reedbeck   I should stop at every
Note to listen to you. But, my dear,
I must present you to his Grace. I'd forgotten
We were not in heaven. Your Grace—this—
This is—

Duke   Steady, Reedbeck.
Let me dry your eyes. Dear man, these tears are something
Remarkably like champagne.

Reedbeck   No doubt they are.
My daughter: his Grace the Duke of Altair.

Duke You have made your father as happy as if his heart
Were breaking. And isn't it likely you're going to make
Other's happy as well? We have only autumn
To offer you, England's moist and misty devotion,
But spring may come in time to reconcile you
If you'll wait so long.

Perpetua   I need no reconciling.
I was born and grew in this green and pleasant aquarium,
And I've spent four days on a wicked October sea
For love of recollected mildew
And my dear frog-father; only I'd scarcely expected
Quite so much impenetrable murk
In the middle of morning. Surely there must be something
Out of sorts about your daylight?

Duke   Nothing
Which time won't mend. But, first, let me introduce—
Ah, they've left us! Hilda and Rosabel

Have passed away with no last word. They always
Bore themselves with the true brevity of empires.
But here is Mrs Dill, more universe
Than empire, less conquered but more embracing.

Jessie I'm very pleased to meet you. Your father loves you
With every word in the language.

Duke   And this, Miss Reedbeck,
Is my first youth, my younger days: the Marquis
Of Charlock.

Edgar   You're a kind of legend with us here,
But the truth is better.

Perpetua   I'll tell you the truth:
I'm very happy this morning; I'm really out
Of prison.

Reedbeck   Of prison, my darling? Why do you say
Of prison?

Perpetua   I mean, of course, the boat was a prison
And the frowning sea was Dartmoor.

Duke   To refresh you
There's wine in the bottle, cider from the wood,
Biscuits in the barrel; and there you can see
Our English sun, convalescent after passing
Through the valley of the shadow of the moon.

Perpetua So that was why I had to search my way
Up the stairs in gloom. How far off is the sun?

Duke The best part of ninety-three million miles.

Perpetua You would hardly think it could matter.

Edgar   What will you drink,
Miss Reedbeck?

Perpetua   Something of England, the cider, presently.
I'm so at peace, though I still can feel
The lunge of the sea. Your floor isn't meant to sway?

Duke The floor is battering at your feet like Attila
With a horde of corybantic atoms,
And travelling at eighteen miles a second,

But it cannot be said to sway.

Jessie   That would be much
Too easy.

Duke   Our stability is a matter
For surprise.

Reedbeck   I feel the terrible truth of that.
Even now, for example, when I see my Perpetua
Sitting like a girl on a swing on an Easter Monday
Under a Wedgwood sky, I can feel my heart—

Perpetua That's just what it's like, a girl on a swing.

Reedbeck   My heart
Knocking most anxiously against the future,
As though afraid to be alone with the present time:
Ready, really, for almost any disaster
Rather than this unsteady tight-rope of joy
I'm walking on now. Are you ill, perhaps? Is that it?
Have you come home for your health?

Perpetua   I've come home to be home.
A pigeon's return—just so simple, Poppadillo.
I wanted to stand where I first grew, and to have
My roots and my branches all in one place together.
And that's no curious thing. Here, swinging
On my swing, with the Atlantic foam still racing
Under my eyelids, I seem at rest already.
And so I sent no word to say I was coming,
Because, in the sense that means the most,
I was here all the time.

Edgar   And so you emerged
Like Venus from the sea.

Perpetua   But sicker.

Reedbeck   What
Shall I do for my returning Mayflower
Suppose she is disappointed in the land
Her roots are in?

Perpetua   You needn't be afraid.
If this is still an island
Enclosed in a druid circle of stony sea.
As misty as it was that chilly Thursday

When I was born to the wilting of plovers
And the smell of a saturation of hops,
Then I'm safely and happily home.

Jessie   Here's to your happiness,
Dear; God save the King, and a mild winter.

Reedbeck Your happiness, my dear.

Edgar   Happiness, Miss Reedbeck.

Duke I should like you to offer Miss Reedbeck an apple, Edgar.

Edgar Anything except an apple, father.
I will offer her
The cloudy peach, the bristling pineapple,
The dropsical pear, the sportive orange,
Apricot, sloe, King William, or a carillon
Of grapes, but not, as God's my judge, an apple.

Duke Then, as Paris abdicates, I must offer
The sweet round robin fruit myself—
(*He holds an apple up between his fingers*)
The green sphere the myth of the word began in,
Which Melanion let fall, delaying
Mercurial Atalanta—

Perpetua whips a very small pistol from a pig-skin holster at her belt. She shoots and shatters the apple. There is an incredulous, shaken silence

Perpetua I—I'm terribly sorry. That was thoughtless of me.
Perhaps you wanted to eat it.

Duke   There are others;
Nature is pleased to give us more. And you
Have been very good; you let me keep my fingers.

Reedbeck Only by the mercy of God! My dear girl,
My dear girl! What in the world possessed you?
You might have been the death of him!

Perpetua   No, it was quite safe.
To please, I always aim. But that, I agree,
Is no excuse. It was dreadful, and shameful of me.
I was thinking of something else, or else
It would never have happened.

Rosabel enters followed by Hilda

Rosabel   What was it? We heard a sound
   Like a shot!

Reedbeck   Good gracious, a *sound* like a shot!

Hilda Is no one hurt?

Duke   An apple came to grief
   As apples must.

Edgar   One pip too many.

Jessie   And nobody
   Was more surprised than the Duke.

Reedbeck   Oh, yes, I think so,
   I think my surprise can hardly have been bettered
   Except, no doubt, by the apple. And I'm still
   Anchored in amazement, I have to confess.

Perpetua I also have to confess; I see I must.
   I thought I could come back again to England
   And slip into this new beginning, silently.
   But now the pistol has gone off; the silence anyway
   Is well and truly broken, and so I'll explain,
   Though the explanation, I'm afraid, will seem
   As wild as the shot.

Reedbeck   What can it be? Be quick
   And tell me.

Perpetua   I've latterly been in prison. But not
   For what we should call a crime.

Reedbeck   They put you in prison
   Without rhyme or reason?

Perpetua   There may have been
   A little rhyme. I was thought to be unsafe
   For democracy, because I broke, or shot,
   Or burnt, a good many things, or rather—and this
   Is the reason—a bad many things: the unsightly,
   The gimcrack, the tedious, the hideous, the spurious,
   The harmful. Not I alone, of course;
   We were all students, and called ourselves
   The Society for the Desecration
   Of Ancient and Modern Monumental Errors.

We destroyed, or tried to destroy, whatever we loathed
As bad.

Rosabel You simply went and destroyed them? You took
The courage into your hands, and destroyed them?
That sounds like a way of living life indeed!

Perpetua Why, no, I think it was only exasperation.
And then most of us were jailed for it.
And while I was inside I began to realize
It was all a futility.
The more we destroyed, the worse the bad sprang up.
And I thought and I thought, what is the purpose of me?
What can I reasonably do in the world?
I was wearing the prison drab. My name was a number.
Inside or outside the prison, Perpetua
(I thought) you're nobody, you're everybody's colour.
First of all you have to make good
Before there's a hope that you can break the bad.
And so I came home to England to look at myself
And see what there was I could conjure out of myself.
(*She offers the pistol to the Duke*)
I'd better surrender this. I only kept it
For a kind of memento. And I apologize
Again for destroying the apple. Still half at sea
As I am, it appeared to be, in a misty way,
Like a threat to my new-come freedom.

Duke I hope you will think so again, some other time.

Rosabel (*taking the pistol*)
May I have it, to remind me of what you have said?
It has meant a great deal to me.

Duke (*taking it from her*)   Caps for you,
Dear Rosabel, not bullets. I'll have it
Filled for your next big scene.

A gong booms from below

Edgar Luncheon! Can we be supposed to eat
On a day when the sun is drowned by the moon,
And apples meet such a strange end?

Duke I see nothing strange. If we can move and talk
Under the sun at all, we must have accepted
The incredible as commonplace, long ago;
And even the incredible must eat.
Shall we go down?

CURTAIN

SCENE 2

The Temple of the Ancient Virtues, beside the ducal lake. That afternoon

Dominic and Perpetua are there

Dominic You haven't spoken for three and a half minutes.

Long pause

>   Four minutes. This is the most pregnant pause
>   Since darkness was on the face of the deep. I suppose
>   You think I shouldn't have told you.

Perpetua   Oh, yes, you should.

Dominic It was better than leaving you in a fool's paradise,
>   You must admit.

Perpetua   I could be twice as silent
>   For seven times as long.

Dominic   Well, then you shall be.
>   I know myself how the shock stuns one.

Perpetua   No shock
>   At all. I was able to believe you at once.
>   Poppadillo has the most beguiling
>   Jackdaw look about him. But you think
>   He wouldn't be happy in prison?

Dominic   He wouldn't, but what
>   Difference does that make? Would you be able
>   To look anyone in the face, with a father jailed?

Perpetua Oh, yes, if he were comfortable. But I think
>   He might feel shut in. No, Dominic, I'm sure
>   You're right. If someone has to go to prison,
>   I must.

Dominic You? What can you possibly mean?

Perpetua I heard you say, perhaps it might have been
>   Six minutes ago, if I made myself agreeable
>   The Duke (you said) being much in that mind at the moment
>   Might, with any luck, be inclined to marry me,
>   And no gentleman (you added) would incriminate
>   His father-in-law. And I agree with you,

And I see my carefree hours already numbered,
My freedom of choice and my individual day.
I'm no longer a woman after my own heart.
Broad cupid's arrows on my wedding veil.
But still, Dominic, for my father's sake
Not ours, I mean to try.

Dominic   God bless you, then,
And God speed you, and thank God I can breathe again.
And a coronet's no martyrdom, particularly
When it sits on a man whom women find easy to like.

Perpetua I wonder how many women have stood perplexed
And plagued in this temple, two whole centuries of them,
Looking out this way, on the same view
Of the metal rusting year. Lemon, amber,
Umber, bronze and brass, oxblood, damson,
Crimson, scalding scarlet, black cedar,
And the willow's yellow fall to grace.

Dominic Do you have to be so melancholy? Everything
Is better now. Though there is still the anxiety
Whether you can prepossess him before he strikes.

Perpetua Oh, yes, there is that anxiety still.
Here comes the straying lamb who gave us life.

Dominic Don't pamper him. We have to make him realize
He's been sinning all this while.

Perpetua   He looks worried
As though he knew it already.

Reedbeck enters out of breath

Reedbeck   So here—here—
You are. I wondered, missed you, but luckily caught
Sight of you going down through the trees. I lost
My hat on the way; it blew (oh, what a gasping old fellow)
Off, blew off; now upside down on the water
Among the *Alisma Plantago-aquatica*.
Didn't think I should have enough breath to say so.

Perpetua Try only breathing, for a time; that's always
Nice.

Dominic What was the hurry? Did you think I was going
To throw her in the water?

Reedbeck   Among the *Alisma*
Plantago-aquatica. Has he been talkin to you?
He's not as fond of me as either of us
Would like.

Perpetua   I've been hearing unimaginable
Things about you.

Reedbeck   Yes, the imagination
Is a frail craft, soon capsizes, quite understand.
Now this, my dear, called sometimes the Temple
Of the Ancient Virtues, and at other times
The White Temple, both because it is white
And because it was designed by Martin White
In seventeen hundred and ninety-three, was erected
By the third Duke of Altair for his wife Claire
For her use when she played the part of the Delphic Oracle,
A way she had of informing the Duke of her pregnancy,
Which she did on twenty-seven separate occasions.

Perpetua Tell me why you've been cheating the Duke,
There's a good boy. What made you do it?

Reedbeck   I hope
I've done nothing so monosyllabic as to cheat.
A spade is never so merely a spade as the word
Spade would imply.

Dominic   One's helpless to help him.

Perpetua Poppadillo, suppose I put it this way:
What made you supercherify with chousery
The Duke?

Reedbeck   That might be said to—that perhaps
Is not an unfair expression. And I say in reply
The reason was the fading charm of the world.
The banquet of civilization is over—

Perpetua   Shall we call it
The groaning board?

Reedbeck   You may call it what you will.
With a little wealth to do it I should like to perform
The grace after the meat, a last gentlemanly,
Valedictory grace: a grace for departing grace
(Is that not rather good?):
The spacious lawns of life are being

Inevitably ploughed, and we don't know, we really
Don't know, what's going to be sown there.
Dignity has dropped upon all fours.
Indeed there's hardly to be seen
One intense perpendicular
In all the streets of men. Someone, you know,
Someone must keep alive that quality
Of living which separates us from the brutes;
And I have proposed it should be I.

Dominic It should be me.

Reedbeck   Beloved boy,
It would be delightful if you thought so.

Perpetua I understand so far; I only wonder
Why the Duke has to be ... out of pocket.

Reedbeck I care so much for civilization,
Its patrician charm, its grave nobility;
He cares so little. Therefore certain eccentric
Means have had to be taken for splendid ends.
It's true I have overlaid the Law
With a certain transposition; we might
Call this process Reedbequity. But what
A gain to the world.

Dominic   Do you hear that, Perpetua?
He even unblushingly gives our name
To his wicked practices!

Perpetua   Dominic wants us all
To be good. Perhaps if you had gone to the Duke
And explained all this, he would have eased the path
To Reedbequity without the bother of iniquity.
Don't you think he might?

Reedbeck   My dear, I've never believed
In the equal distribution of property.
I only think it can have more beauty
In my hands than in his. But that would have been
A most impertinent thing to say to him.

Perpetua We must keep you from harm. Heydee,
I'm not to be myself, I see.
I'm sad to see myself go;
But I was only promise, after all,
And the world can't live on that.

Reedbeck Have you something that worries you? I believe
  I've made you discontented with me, on a day
  Which should have turned out so glorious, and now
  I don't know *where* we are.

Dominic   It's only a step
  From where you are, father, to where you will be
  If we can't prevent it. You'll discover
  Civilization is sadly dwindled when
  You make your way to prison. Here's the Duke.
  Be cheerful, if you can, Perpetua.

Perpetua   My smile
  Will be like the glint of handcuffs, but he's very
  Welcome to it. Sing out a joke, Dominic,
  In your merry way.

Dominic   Ssh!

Perpetua   That's a most promising
  Start to a conversation. There must be a joke
  Lying about somewhere, even when the leaves are falling.

Reedbeck Something about . . . when the leaves in Eden fell . . .

Perpetua Dear Poppadillo; thank you.

Reedbeck   Was it at all
  Serviceable?

Perpetua   It had a kind of ancient virtue,
  Proper for this time and temple, yes.

  The Duke enters, carrying a bow and quiver

Duke May your little girl come out and play, Reedbeck?
  Daylight is short, and becoming always shorter.
  But there's the space for an arrow or two between
  Now and the sunset.

Perpetua   I've never handled a bow.
  How shall I manage?

Duke   Beautifully.
  The light will hang fire to see you; you might
  Even hear the flash of the foliage
  Where Artemis parts the leaves to patronize

And praise you; but take no notice, and watch what you're doing,
And do what I tell you.

Perpetua   Implicitly.

Duke   Take notice
Of the excellent marksmanship of the year, whose arrow
Singing from the April bow crossed over the width
Of summer straight for the gold, where now, if you look,
You will see it quivering.

Perpetua   The year has a world of experience.
But still, show me; and I'll try not to shame the shades
Of all the duchesses and ladies
Who played on these lawns before.

Duke Be confident; and, if you miss,
The fashion of the game will be to miss,
Until you change your mind and hit.

*He begins to instruct her in the use of the bow, holding it with her, and
speaking low into her ear, so that Reedbeck and Dominic cannot hear*

And then, Perpetua, to-night
If a clear sky inclines you to it, and the heavens
Remain suspended, how would it be
If we trained the telescope on the infinite
And made what we could of what we could see of it?
Are you still as interested as you were
This morning?

Perpetua   Yes I come from a city. The stars
Are new to me.

Duke   They shall answer you
By numbers. But we'll not tell the world
What we mean to do. There's a little tension to-day
Already, nerves perhaps not ready to accept
The quiet session of scientific study
You and I propose. So let's be as mute
As we're mutable, and avoid misapprehension.

Perpetua I—if so—if so—yes, very well.

Duke You can tell the world you need a long night of sleep.

Perpetua Yes, yes, I can. But here's the good afternoon light
Fading to waste unless we make use of it.

Duke I know that thought so well. Come on, then,
    Let the trial begin.

Perpetua   Watch me, Poppadillo.
    Come and judge what a huntress I should make,
    What a rival for Artemis, and what chance Actaeon
    Would have if I pursued him.

*   The Duke and Perpetua exit*

Reedbeck   She really makes me
    Respectful of astrology; it must
    Have been the arrangement of stars she was born under.
    It couldn't have been all me and her mother. Why,
    I couldn't even dream so beautifully,
    Let alone propagate. It must have been
    The state of the zodiac when she was conceived.
    But even so, I was there, and that in itself
    Is remarkable. What did you say to her, Dominic;
    What did you say to her?

Dominic   I simply told her
    You were crooked.

Reedbeck   And then she said?

Dominic   She said
    She was not surprised.

Reedbeck   Oh. *I* should have been;
    It would have seemed like a thunder clap to *me*.
    But you've made her feel differently towards me,
    You've sent me off on my own again. And what
    Did she mean by "sad to see herself go", and "not
    To be herself any more?" What made her say that?
    Was something agreed between you?

Dominic   I made a point.

Reedbeck What point, now what point?

Dominic   I made the suggestion
    She might like to marry the Duke, and save you that way.

Reedbeck You—said—such a—thing? You dared
    To consider selling your sister? You,
    Sprung from my loins, and so utterly
    Unprincipled?

Dominic   That sounds most convincing,
Coming from you!

Reedbeck   Poor little girl, poor
Little girl. But I'll intervene—*inter venio*,
Yes—though I can't relieve her
Of her inhuman brother.

Dominic   Or her dishonest
Father.

Reedbeck (*shaking him, in a sudden burst of rage*)
            You're a vain, vexing, incomprehensible,
Crimping, constipated duffer. What's your heart?
All plum duff? Why do I have to be
So inarticulate? God give me a few
Lithontriptical words! You grovelling little
Gobemouche!

Dominic   Stop it, Father, stop it at once!

Reedbeck You spigoted, bigoted, operculated prig!

Jessie enters with a writing case and pen

Jessie Am I in the way? I came to write a letter.

*Reedbeck releases Dominic suddenly, and Dominic trips and falls sprawling on
the floor*

Reedbeck I was having a word with my son.

Jessie (*to Dominic*)   How do you do?
Please don't bother to get up.

Reedbeck   You're very welcome
To write your letter. I don't wish to shake him
Any more. But if you hadn't come in
I think I should have gone on shaking him
Until I couldn't see him.

Jessie   He would still
Have been there, of course. When my mother used to shake me
It always gave me hiccups, and then I was given
Peppermint on sugar to cure them. If only your son
Had hiccups, and you had peppermint and sugar,
Mr Reedbeck, everything would seem different.

Dominic I have to leave you. I'm afraid my father
Must be feeling very chastened and confused.

Dominic exits

Jessie It was lovely exercise for both of you.

Reedbeck It did no good. I've only shaken my own
Composure.

Jessie   Sit down, Mr Reedbeck, and let it settle.
I have to get a few lines off every day
To my father, eighty-seven. He can't read a word
Of my handwriting, and doesn't try, but he likes
The postman.

Reedbeck   Well, I'll leave you, then;
I won't stop and hinder you. I suppose
That action of mine, that sudden accession of rage,
Wasn't in the nicest mood of civilization?
And yet I don't at all feel like apologizing,
I don't feel at all like apologizing. Would you apologize?

Jessie I'm sorry, I was trying to think how to begin
So that Dad won't mind he can't read it.

Reedbeck Well, I won't stop and hinder you now,
But I should be very upset if I proved to be
Nothing but a barbarian after all,
A barbarian dreaming of the higher excellences.
But I won't stop and hinder you.

Hilda enters

                        Mrs Dill
Is trying to write a letter. We mustn't hinder her.

Reedbeck exits

Hilda I see Hereward has made another backward
Flight into his heyday. It's a handsome thing
To see him so happy, but are we so happy for the girl?

Jessie Doesn't she like playing at bows and arrows?

Hilda She does, no doubt, but—may I interrupt you?

Jessie   I'm only
  Writing a letter when nothing else occurs to me;
  I like to talk.

Hilda   Because of the strange business
  Of the eclipse this morning, and what went on,
  We've been thrown into each other's confidence
  Unexpectedly soon. And for my part
  I think I'm thankful. I've always hidden more
  Than was good for me, hoping in that way
  To make my life seem pleasant to everyone,
  But who should care? So I've lost the habit
  Of daring to ask myself what I do, or why.
  Why did I come here to-day, and what did I expect?
  And why did he ever invite us here together?
  I know him painstakingly enough
  To be sure it was kindly meant; it couldn't have been
  To watch our faces fall.

Jessie   I like being here
  So much I never even wondered.

Hilda   There
  Was still something in me to be hurt,
  Which a little surprised me. And then
  Reedbeck's daughter came, as though to show
  How the years had gone by for us
  But not for him, as though the old
  Magician in his blood was bound to draw us
  Into that revealing circle. But I sigh
  For her, as once I sighed for myself; and if
  I knew how, I should tell her how lightly he flies.

Jessie   And then
  You must tell her how nicely he alights.
  That's important, too.
  I should let them be, because be they will.

Hilda When I first met him, I remember, he seemed
  At once to give my spirits a holiday,
  Though (like a first holiday abroad) almost too unlike
  The daily round of the roundabout life I led—
  And lead still, O my heavens —which had, and has,
  All the appearance of movement without covering
  Any ground whatsoever. I know I have
  No particular heights or depths myself;
  No one who thought me ordinary or dull
  Would be far wrong. But even I despair

For Roderic, my husband, who really is
The height of depth, if it doesn't sound unkind
To say so: not deep depth, but a level depth
Of dullness. Once he had worn away the sheen
Of his quite becoming boyhood, which made me fancy him,
There was nothing to be seen in Roderic
For mile after mile after mile, except
A few sheeplike thoughts nibbling through the pages
Of a shiny weekly, any number of dead pheasants,
Partridges, pigeons, jays, and hares,
An occasional signpost of extreme prejudice
Marked "No thoroughfare", and the flat horizon
Which is not so much an horizon
As a straight ruled line beyond which one doesn't look.

Jessie Keep him warm and fed. They bloom
Once in seven years.

Hilda   Not Roderic.

Edgar enters, carrying a bow and quiver

Edgar   Isn't it strange?
For the first time in my young life
I'm jealous of my father. I thought I'd better
Mention it before I begin to brood.

Hilda Jealous of him, why?

Edgar   To me he's a man
Once and for all; once, once only,
And certainly for all. And any man
Who has to follow him (me, for instance)
Feels like the lag-last in a cloud of locusts:
By the time I come to a tree it's as bare
As a hat stand. Talent, conversation, wit,
Ease, and friendliness are all swallowed up
In advance. And just at present
I feel depressed about it.

Hilda   Now, take heart.
You have those virtues, too. There's room for both of you.

Edgar Not, I think, at the moment.

Jessie   Do you mean
Only two can play at bows and arrows?

Hilda I think at the moment it's greatly important
    There *should* be room for both of you. Suppose
    You make a bid for it. Why not?
    Nothing hinders you except weakness of hope,
    And that's ridiculous. We'll go together.
    Mrs Dill wants to write a letter.

Jessie   Never mind;
    Everything writes itself in time.

Bates enters

Bates It's Mrs Taylor-Snell I'm looking for;
    Oh, that's right, lady, you're here. I have
    A message to give you, they said; prompto.
    On the telephone it come. It's not so nice
    As you might like to have it, but it's not so bad.
    It seems there's been a bit of a accident,
    And they'd be glad if you could make it convenient
    To find your way back 'ome.

Hilda   Roderic!

Bates Whoever it is, missie, you're not to worry.
    Your old man has got hisself throwed off his horse,
    Hunting little rabbits and uvver breeders.
    Now, now, lady, you never know,
    It may only be a front toof a bit loose.

Hilda Didn't they say what the injury was?

Bates Took a bit of a toss, come a bit of a purler,
    What Jack and Jill done; don't you worry, lady.

Hilda I can't help worrying, dear Bates. (*To Jessie*) I'll go
    Without saying good-bye to Hereward. There's no reason
    Why anyone's afternoon should suffer,
    Except mine; and later I'll telephone
    And tell you what has happened.

Jessie   It's wretched for you,
    It's really wretched for you; I'm awfully sorry.
    What would you like me to do?

Hilda   Nothing, except
    To forget I laughed at him. I have my car;
    I can slip away easily.

Edgar   I'll run on ahead
And get the car started for you.

Hilda   No.
Thank you, but I'd rather go quietly alone.
If you want to do something for me, put your shoulders
To your father, and make yourself your own success.
Goodbye.

Edgar   Good-bye, good luck.

Jessie   I expect you'll find
It's something nice and simple like a collar-bone.

Hilda exits

Oh, please God, make it a collar-bone. She turned
So pale and unhappy, poor lamb.

Bates I wouldn't have anything happen to that one
It's a pity we can't do something to oblige her.
But there's that uvver one, Fleming she says she's called:
Flaming nuisance, I reply: what about her,
Eh, miss? What's she doing snooping
About the east wing all the afternoon? I tell you,
Miss, I know an undesirable character
When I see one; I've been one myself for years.

Jessie And look how we love you. So don't you have
Nasty thoughts about Miss Fleming, who is not
Undesirable at all. And go away
Like a good boy, and let me write my letter.

Bates I just fought you might like the opinion of a expert.
(*He begins wandering away*)
But don't let's say anyfing good about
Captain Fussing Reddleman, lord of the kitchens.
He can go and tame his lions on some uvver poor bastard's mug.
I prefers to keep mine natural.

Bates exits

Edgar I wonder if I should.

Jessie   If you should what?

Edgar From here I think I could send an arrow right past him
  Into the target.

Jessie   If you think you can, then do.

*Edgar takes an arrow, fits it in his bow, and shoots. A distant cry of
remonstrance from the Duke*

Edgar Oh, that was very beautiful. I enjoyed that
  Extremely.

Jessie   What did you do? Did I encourage you
  To be mischievous? I was thinking about my letter.
  You might have shot your father.

Edgar   I jolly nearly
  Did. But my arrows, I never quite know why,
  Have a considerate way of going where
  I mean them to go, which was nearer the gold than his.
  He's probably shooting not so well
  To give Perpetua some encouragement.
  When I come to think of it, that shot of mine
  Was taking a very easy advantage.

Jessie I shouldn't say easy, twice the distance off.
  And as you didn't kill anybody, I may say
  I think it was splendid, and I think perhaps
  You should do it more often.

  The Duke enters

Duke What, by Saint Sebastian's groin,
  Do you think you're up to? Edgar, for goodness' sake!

Edgar I was drawing a bow at a venture, Father.

Duke   So
  I thought. But remember what damage was done to Sir Lancelot
  By an arrow in the buttocks. Did I beget you
  To be shot from behind?

Edgar   I'm extremely sorry,
  But you took a step to the south.

Duke   Am I never to move?

Edgar Oh, yes, Father, but the other way, or any way
  Except between me and where I aim.

Duke   I hope
  I'm being patient. I had quite supposed
  The contest was between Miss Reedbeck and me.

Edgar When all the time it was really between you
  And your loving son; or so my hackles tell me.

Duke Ah—! Now I see;
  Your days are starting to press upon me,
  You who were always so unassuming and easy.
  But not this time. No, I'm sorry,
  Not this time, Edgar.

Edgar   It is this time.
  I'm sorry, too, but it is this time. You've had
  A long innings, and a summer of splendid outings,
  And now I must ask you, Father, not to monopolize
  Every heart in the world any longer.

Jessie   Excuse me
  Worrying you, but how do you spell epidemic?
  Two *p's* and two *m's*?

Edgar   I'd forgotten we weren't alone.

Duke We're alone with Jessie; nothing could be happier.
  One *p*, one *m*. If the generations join
  In a life-and-death struggle under your feet
  Don't let it, Jessie, disturb your spelling.

Jessie One *p*, one *m*. Quite enough, when you look at it.

Duke Now listen, Edgar, take nothing for granted,
  Not even my flair for breaking into love;
  You're apprehensive far too soon. The field,
  If not entirely yours, is not entirely mine:
  I am as innocently there
  As an old warhorse put out to grass:
  My equine equability is pastoral to a fault.

Edgar But when you're grazing you're irresistible;
  Buttercups and daisies fall to your fetlocks in swathes;
  I've seen it happen. And between this morning's eclipse
  And this afternoon you've lost the autumnal look
  Which was such a comfort to me; I see you have
  The appearance of a very mild March day.
  And what does a boy do then?

Duke   Aren't you being
Just a thought parricidal for a fine afternoon?

Edgar Oh, God, I love you like the rest of them.
I'm only asking you to forgo yourself
This once, to suspend your animation
For a few short months, for my sake.

Duke   Edgar,
I mean to be a good father to you, but
A good father must be a man. And what
Is a man? Edgar, what is a man? O
My man-child, what in the world is a man?
Speaking for myself, I am precisely that question:
I exist to know that I exist
Interrogatively. But what gives birth
To a question? A desire to be answered. A question
Desires, as a man must desire, as I
Desire. That, at least, you'll allow me.
You wouldn't have your father merely rhetorical.

Edgar Not at all, but—

Duke   But what is the mark of the question?
What is the note of this interrogation?
Loneliness. The note my son, is loneliness.
Over all the world
Men move unhoming, and eternally
Concerned: a swarm of bees who have lost their queen,
Nothing else is so ill at ease. We know
How patiently the toad suns on the stone,
How the indolent fish waves its tail in time
With the waving weed. If a pulse was in the stone,
And the stone grew moist, and the toad petrified,
Patience would still be as patient in the sun.
Or if the weed wove its way up river
To breed, and the fish waved green and still,
The water would never wonder: all
Is at one with the rest.
And the trees, when the weather is waking, quicken without
Question, their leaves assemble in a perfect faith
Of summer; and so with all the world's life,
Except ours. We can hear the lyric lark
Flaking its limit of heaven from a cloud,
And see the self-assimilated cat,
The adaptable chameleon, and the mole
Rubbing along companionably
With the obliging earth. But where, O Edgar,
Is an element compatible with *us*?

Edgar Would you mind if I reminded you, father,
What we were talking about when you started talking?

Duke Thank you, but I know: your wish to remove me.
But if being alive is a question, heaven-bent
For an answer, and the question is a man's
Estrangement in a world
Where everything else conforms, how should I dare
To suspend myself for a day, or even an hour,
When that hour might ravish me
Into a complete, unsolitary life,
Where happiness leaves no room for the restless mind
And I, as unlaborious
As a laburnum tree, hang in caresses of gold.

Edgar And what do I hang in?

Duke   You hang in abeyance, Edgar.
If I should die, with the great question unanswered,
I leave myself in you to ask it still.
But this is all academic. The field is still open.

Jessie I always think "niece" is such a difficult word.

Duke *I* before *E*, except after *C*. And so,
Edgar, let nothing dismay you—

Jessie   Except
In the case of "neigh", that humorous noise of a horse.

Perpetua enters

Perpetua Is archery all over? I went to the lake
And tried to spear fish with an arrow, but I'm tired
Of that.

Duke   Edgar, I'm nowhere to be seen;
For all the personality I exert
You might never have had a father; advance, advance,
You son of a cipher.

Perpetua   Could we not all shoot together?

Edgar Miss Reedbeck—

Perpetua   Perpetua.

Edgar   Yes, Perpetua,
   This is All Hallowe'en. Tonight half England
   Will be dancing in memory of a world they don't remember.
   The sky will very likely be black with broomsticks.
   There's a dance on in the Old Woolmarket
   At Mordenbury. Will you come?

Perpetua (*glancing towards the Duke*) All Hallowe'en.
   I should have liked it dearly, but tonight—

Edgar You've made some other plan.

Perpetua   No, no.

Edgar Then come. Meet England first among the wisps
   Of magic we still possess. Will you, Perpetua?

Perpetua If I dared to trust my eyes and my feet
   To be lively, so long after sunset,
   I should say yes willingly. But I must and will
   Sleep early. Four days on the see-saw sea,
   And then such a wave of homecoming, have left me
   Ready to rest. I'm so sorry to refuse.

Edgar Well, I see you must, though I'm very sad you must.
   But if later you should feel revived, or if
   You found you could rest before dinner—

Perpetua It still has to be no, and still I'm sorry.

Edgar I can well imagine how tired you are. You can let
   Your sleep make you a Hallowe'en instead.
   Dreams know where to look for deeper and stronger
   Shadows than I do. Horses, it always seems
   To me, are half a dream, even when
   You have them under your hand, and when I *dream* them
   They tremble and sweat, the caves of their nostrils blowing
   Bright clouds of breath, a foaming sea
   Breaks against their mouths, their flanks are smoking
   Like Abel's fire to heaven, as though
   A dreadful necessity had ridden them hard
   Through the miles of my sleep, all the benighted way
   From legend into life. And then in the morning
   There they are in the stables, waiting to be blessed.

Perpetua Show me these wonders.

Edgar   Now?

Perpetua   Yes, why not now?
  All of us.

Edgar   That goes for you, Papa.

Duke Invisibly I come.

Edgar (*glumly*)   Invisibility
  Makes you look younger than ever.

  Perpetua and Edgar exit

Duke   Jessie,
  Will you make an end of dotting your i's and join us?

Jessie Thank you, dear,
  But I'd like to finish this letter to my father,
  Even though he'll never read it.

Duke   Jessie, my love,
  If he'll never read it, do you have to write so much?

Jessie Well, no, but he lives such a long way out of the village
  I like to make it worth the postman's while.

  Rosabel enters

Duke Rosabel, where have you been mooning
  All the long afternoon? Come with your friends
  And look at horses. Edgar is showing Miss Reedbeck
  Round the stables.

Rosabel   Yes, yes, I may follow you—
  When do you mean to show her how to observe
  The stars through your telescope? Is it tonight?

Duke No, not tonight; sometime, perhaps, or perhaps
  Never; who can say?

Rosabel   But *you* will be there, I suppose
  Who is it that's mooning then? And all night long?
  And making the world look small and apologetic
  And as good as unpopulated? I hate your telescope!

Duke So you have said. Don't let it obsess you
  Look up, Mrs Siddons, it's easy enough

To see over the top of a telescope. So try,
Or you'll soon make yourself ill. Anyway
I'm washing my hands of all the sky tonight,
And I'm going early to bed.

The Duke exits

Rosabel Yes, I see. I just wondered ...
What am I to do? I came here, quite easy-hearted,
Thinking he recalled what used to matter to him.
But then I was sent spinning.
I was lined up like a woman at a hiring fair.
I know I should just walk away, as I almost did.
It's his own life he is making. Or diminishing,
That's what haunts me.
Since his wife died, through all these years,
Nothing has been of much worth to him, it has all
Been a pretty trivial game, using this very
Precious existence as something to kill time with.
The willing heart has gone out of him.
I know it's nobody else's business,
The way he prefers to live. What right have I
To think I can change it? but if it's wounding him
As gravely as I think it is, is love
To do nothing at all?

Jessie Sorry, dear, I wasn't taking notice
Of what you were saying.

Rosabel   He's absolutely right
When he said it's become an obsession with me; it's a loathing of all
His astronomical works and what they stand for.
It's the bloody world he should be looking at,
The world around him, the people near him. Oh, well.
Yes, me too, if you like. The girl Perpetua—
Did you hear what she said about destroying things
That were sad and insufferable?
It's as though, almost as though she had come here
To show me what I must do, whatever the cost of it.

Jessie Listen, love, you'll be driving yourself silly.
Look at me: I've gone and put Surrey
When I mean Suffolk ... You know, from some points of view
He's as kind as anybody living, don't worry so.

Rosabel And I mustn't be afraid of doing it, mustn't be afraid.
It would mean, you see, releasing a thunderbolt on him.
I'm not sure if I've got the heart for it; I hope so.

Jessie Now I wonder who's the most likely person to have a stamp?

Curtain

ACT II

The Observatory Room. That night

The Duke is lying on the day-bed in the dark

Perpetua enters. The light from the corridor follows her a little way into the room. She stands uncertain. The Duke speaks from the darkness

Duke And Endymion, when the moon had borne him
　Fifty daughters, was rewarded with
　An eternal siesta; his breast and belly rose
　And fell like the sea; his breath played
　All day with the motes of the dust,
　While all about him suffered, withered, and crumbled
　Into the dust his breath played with; only,
　Between the slats of his perfect sleep
　Came little slants of sun, and they were muddy
　With the hard wading of humanity;
　This made him change his position slightly,
　And that stirred up the scent of the thyme which made
　His unimpassioned bed.

Perpetua　　　　　　　　It's rather frightening
　When a dark room starts to speak.

Duke　　　　　　　　　　　My original
　Syntax, like original sin, grows vastier
　In the dark. Come in.

Perpetua　　　　　What does your legend mean?

Duke It means, Perpetua, we're all as well
　As can be expected. Does anyone know you're here?

Perpetua No one.

Duke　　　　They would think I meant to love you.
　I wonder if I mean any such thing.
　We'll make some light. Matches?

Perpetua   No.

Duke No, here are some.
  (*He lights an oil lamp*)
                              This was the first
  Astonishment of creation; after that
  Came the frenzy of which you and I
  Are the humble result.
  God gave way
  To hallucinations; you and me again.
  Would you like a drink?

Perpetua   Thank you. Tell me, as one
  Hallucination to another, what
  Happiness do you get up here with your telescope?

Duke I can't remember. That's a handsome moth
  Come in to die, two petals, two tendrils,
  And a flake of snow, meticulous, irrelevant,
  Unwise. You came to see my stars. I have them
  Here.

Perpetua I expect you can find your way about them
  Even in the dark. Tell me who it is
  We're trained on now.

Duke   Senator Saturn, white-
  Hot with gravity. His moon, out of love
  For his grey steel brow,
  Streamed away her life into a circle
  Of tormented arms.
  You see how they circle and never touch.
  Saturn is alone, for all their circling round him.

Perpetua And alone so long,
  Alone so long, and now casually
  Descending to us, on a Thursday midnight:
  Saturn, who once glinted in the glass
  Of Ariadne's mirror at the moment
  When she died and melted out of Naxos.

Duke Ariadne died in childbirth. One
  Life put the other out. It was Edgar's mode
  Of entrance. Where in the sky shall we go to now?

Perpetua Wherever you may like to take me. I'm
  A stranger here.

Duke   She died a girl in love,
And I went on in love without her
For longer than was fair. But this is not
Astronomy.

Perpetua   Astrology, then. You can't
Throw someone against the sky and not expect
A certain vapour of magic to condense
In moisture on their lashes. Let me believe
For a little while in man's ordeal by star
And tell me your own. I want to hear it.

Duke Isn't it a strange love, Perpetua,
That will never, can never, know what it was?
Death chose to interrupt us while we were still
Careening together high above the spires
Of common sense. And so what modulation
Would have come, how soon, how scaling down,
Is never to be known. And I can never tell
Whether a love, which was haled away
While it still was hale, was all and more
Of love than I could expect again: or if
The one twin-hearted permanence
Was waiting somewhere ahead. That has always
Perplexed me. What have I been doing, since
She died? Making do because the best
Was done? Or have I been turning head by head
To find the face which, willingly
I should never let pass? For a long while now
I've been thinking the first, but to-day
The question seems to have sprung into life again.

Perpetua With your mind so full of inquiry, I'm surprised
You've had any time for love.

Duke   It takes no time
It's on us while we walk, or in mid-sentence,
A sudden hoarseness, enough to choke the sense.
Now isn't that so?

Perpetua   Not so with me.

Duke   You must try
To use longer sentences. Then you would certainly feel
The fumbling in the quiver behind every syllable
And so to the arrow sting, like a sudden
Swerving parenthesis.

Perpetua   Do you think I should?

Duke No doubt of it.

Perpetua   There isn't any reason
   Why a sentence, I suppose, once it begins,
   Once it has risen to the lips at all
   And finds itself happily wandering
   Through shady vowels and over consonants
   Where ink's been spilt like rivers or like blood
   Flowing for the cause of some half-truth
   Or a dogma now outmoded, shouldn't go
   Endlessly moving in grave periphrasis
   And phrase in linking phrase, with commas falling
   As airily as lime flowers, intermittently,
   Uninterrupting, scarcely troubling
   The mild and fragile progress of the sense
   Which trills trebling like a pebbled stream
   Or lowers towards an oath-intoning ocean
   Or with a careless and forgetful music
   Looping and threading, tuning and entwining,
   Flings a babel of bells, a carolling
   Of such various vowels the ear can almost feel
   The soul of sound when it lay in chaos yearning
   For the tongue to be created; such a hymn
   If not as lovely, then as interminable,
   As restless, and as heartless, as the hymn
   Which in the tower of heaven the muted spheres
   With every rippling harp and windy horn
   Played for incidental harmony
   Over the mouldering rafters of the world,
   Rafters which seldom care to ring, preferring
   The functional death-watch beetle, stark, staccato,
   Economical as a knuckle bone,
   Strict, correct, but undelighting
   Like a cleric jigging in the saturnalia,
   The saturnalia we all must keep,
   Green-growing and rash with life,
   Our milchy, mortal, auroral, jovial,
   Harsh, unedifying world,
   Where every circle of grass can show a dragon
   And every pool's as populous as Penge,
   Where birds, with taffeta flying, scarf the air
   On autumn evenings, and a sentence once
   Begun goes on and on, there being no reason
   To draw to any conclusion so long as breath
   Shall last, except that breath
   Can't last much longer.

Duke   Now point me out the comma
Where you loved me.

Perpetua   Not at any.

Duke   Let me see;
Was there a colon somewhere?

Perpetua   Perhaps one;
But if so we passed it without any trouble
Of any sort.

Duke   Never mind. There are sure
To be other sentences. The little god
Is older than he was, and moves more slowly.

Perpetua Even when he aims at you?

Duke   For me, I'm afraid,
He makes a special effort, shoots
Most generously, and then, poor boy, can't handle
A bow for several weeks.

Perpetua   Why are you so sure
That I must love you?
Be sure of nothing.

Duke Do you know what night this is?

Perpetua   All-Hallows Eve.

Duke All-Hallows Eve. If the earth is ever wise
To magic, this is the night when magic's wisdom
Comes rolling in across our sedate equation.
All the closed hours unlock; the rigorous ground
Grows as soft as the sea, exhaling
The bloom of the dead everywhere. They almost
Live again: as nearly, at least, as we
Can brush on death. And through the night
They trespass agreeably on our time of trespasses,
Molesting the air in a pale, disinterested
Way, until they thankfully notice
The dark is paler, and sigh themselves out again;
Though not before they've planted, as they go,
A seed of chill which grows rapidly
Into a rigid winter where the sun
Can hardly raise himself to make a noon.

But still, that's presently. What's more to our purpose
Is that tonight the gravity of mirrors
Is so potent it can draw the future
Into the glass, and show shadows of husbands
To girls who sit and comb their hair. Suppose
You try it.

Perpetua   I'm two or three centuries
Too late.

Duke   We know nothing yet.
There's the mirror. In your bag no doubt
A comb. And while you comb tradition says
You must eat an apple: though God knows why
Any apple should trust itself between your teeth
After this morning's little episode.
However, here's one intrepid to the core.

Perpetua How old is this mirror? The glass
Is very loath to let me in.

Duke   Eight duchesses
Have rested there in passing, before the glass
Began to cloud; and after that came three
Peering housekeepers, a chambermaid
Who, what with frequent tears and the ageing mirror,
Never saw her face; and me, who by
Much early study have overcome the need
To try.

Perpetua And I am the eight duchesses
And the three housekeepers and the chambermaid
Combing their hair. I am any girl: Perpetua
Perpetual, making no gesture I can call
My own, engraving theirs one lifetime deeper.
Midnight, the apple, and Perpetua
Combing her hair, as all the time she was.

*The Duke quietly crosses the room until his reflection falls into the mirror.
Perpetua's attention is caught: she stares into the glass before she turns
suddenly to look at the Duke*

It seemed to be your son.

Duke   Perpetua,
You must play fair.

Perpetua   You must tell that to the mirror.
The reflection seemed to be Edgar.

Duke   Then the mirror
Is very penetrating. It has seen
How young, to all intents, I am.

Perpetua   I suppose so.
You think there's no magic.

Duke   That's as kind
As anything you've said. I think there *is*
Magic: an old dim-sighted mirror
And a shaded lamp for one genial moment
Raised me out of the falling leaves. A pity
The vision has gone. I'll agree to immortality
If immortality is to be always twenty-five
Seen by a man approaching sixty. The thought
Alone sends me begging to Olympus.
And you, being twenty-five, and looked upon
By me, together we make one golden flesh
For which both worlds, this and the next, will try
To outbid each other, and while the bidding mounts
We'll spend our love between them, disregarding
Both until—

Perpetua   Until, next year,
I am twenty-six.   .

Duke   Which is twenty-five and one more.
I am the one.

Perpetua   It remains for me to love you.

Duke It has always been understood to be so easy.
Why ever should you not? Am I, before
God, too old? Consider the rocks
Of Arizona, and then consider me.
How recently the world has had the pleasure
Of pleasing, the opportunity of knowing me.
Age, after all, is only the accumulation
Of extensive childhood: what we were,
Never what we are. Don't deliver me
Up to my grey hairs.

Perpetua   Them I could certainly
Love. No, it's rather that I wonder
Whether you're not almost too young to be lived with.

Duke When we're married I shall age beside you; forgive me
Loitering now till you draw level.

Perpetua When we're married?

Duke   Are we to be formal?
Should I have asked you first?

Perpetua   Not if you have
Some other way of knowing the answer. Have you?

Duke Perhaps I may pass that question back. Have I?

Perpetua Your Grace—

Duke   Somewhere I have a Christian name.

Perpetua Do you know anything against my father?

Duke In my heart, nothing.
He loves me in his way, and that absolves him
From any defect on earth. No doubt
He'll have to stand in a corner of heaven with his face
To a jasper wall, but here let him thrive.

Perpetua   You mean
You know.

Duke   I know he wishes to make honey.
Any bee would tell you, that's impossible
If clover objects to rape.

Perpetua   So this is how
You know I shall marry you: for Poppadillo's sake?

Duke This is how.

Perpetua   And perhaps it is going to feel
Strange to you at first to know I am not.
No, no, you're mistaken, and I was quite
Mistaken, too! This isn't how I mean
To lose my way, by force of circumstantial
Evidence. When I lose my way I shall lose it
In my own time, and by my own misguided
Sense of direction.

Duke   Planting your own brambles,
Digging your own pitfalls, willing your own
Will-o'-the-wisps, designing
Down to the last detail Perpetua's Folly.

Perpetua Without respect of persons. But do you mean
You have sat perched up here, for months and years,
Your eyes shrewdly glittering with starlight,
Knowing that my father, fifty feet below,
Was being clever in your clover, and you said
Nothing?

Duke   We were being so happy together.
And if I had mentioned it, he would have felt
Obliged to discontinue, which would have been
Immensely sad. And, what is more,
Swarming stars and solitary Duke
Would have been unvisited to-night.

Perpetua How happy do you feel to know you tried
For a bride by this conspiracy of silence?

Duke How happy do you feel to know you were ready
To take a husband to make that silence absolute?

Perpetua I made no pretence of loving you. I was glad
When Edgar came to the mirror; I don't know why.

Duke I seem to have come to the end of myself
Sooner than I expected. So there's to be
No climax and adorable close
With ego agonistes crowned and smiling?
The strange charm of being alive breaks off
Abruptly, with nothing determined, nothing solved,
No absolute anything. I thought this time
The ends of the ring would join. But, no,
I'm back among the fragments.

Perpetua   Is this fair?

Duke How nature loves the incomplete. She knows
If she drew a conclusion it would finish her.
But, O God, for one round Amen!

Perpetua   That only
Comes on judgement day, and so,
As love won't live with judgement, Amen must wait.
Show me one more star and I must go.

Duke I think they're falling.
While I love you without being loved they're sure
To be restive.

Perpetua   When they fall do they scorch the air
In passing? Is that what I can smell?
Something *is* on fire. I can hear the flames
Crunching on the wood.

Duke   Have my almost mindless gardeners
Been suddenly visited by imagination
And lit us a Hallowe'en bonfire?

Perpetua   Why, look, the garden's
Capering with light. The fire is underneath us—
Look! It's the house, this wing of the house is on fire!

Duke Merciful heaven,
Wouldn't you think my blood was warm enough
To get us through a night without encouragement?

Perpetua Shall we be able to get away?

Duke   By all means.
We'll leave the moths to perform whatever
Immolation is necessary. A more
Temperate life is better for us,
And the cooler coast of the garden.
(*He throws open the door and looks on to the stairs*)
Well, here's a riproaring gauntlet to be run
By a couple of God's children.

Perpetua   No! No, no!
Not that way!

Duke   Which other? The only alternative
To downward is upward, and how do you propose
Two such wingless babes as we are—
No, Perpetua; quickly, love, before
The even chance is out of patience with us.

Perpetua No! There's no chance there. You can see
There's no chance there. It's all in the fire,
Every tread of the stairs. What shall we do?
(*She runs to the window and looks down*)
So far away, so far away.

Duke   Trust me;
Try this way in my arms, Perpetua. Hope
Is forlorn, but I'm sure very fond of us.
We'll give her the benefit, shall we, and both be brave?

Perpetua Don't make me. I'd rather jump to the garden, and die
Fair and broken. I'll make my own death
As it suits me.

Duke   That as well? I'm sorry; you can have
Your own way in everything else.

Perpetua   Please.
Please, please, please.

Duke   Well, I see
We've chosen. Hope has got tired of waiting
And taken half the staircase with her. Now,
We'll ring a rescue, and then indulge in the luxury
Of having nothing to do but fold our hands.

He holds her beside him while he uses the telephone

Gently, my dear, you White Queen; nothing
Has hurt us yet. A fire at Stellmere Park.
Two people trapped: neither anxious to die.
I suggest you should make remarkable speed.
God bless you. They didn't wait for blessing.

Perpetua Aren't you desperate, too? Aren't you even afraid?

Duke Why, yes, yes, I have to be; I love myself,
And I shall be sad to say good-bye to myself:
There's no one like me, though so many better.
Will you kiss the last of a singular man?

Perpetua Easily, oh, easily.

Duke   There's always a good thing left
Even when the world would seem to be spent out.
Do you think you love me?

Perpetua   Yes, I love you:
Between the giddiness I love you.

Duke   May it also
Be between my arms? I love my love
With a death because it has no alteration
And no end. This concluding grace, Amen.

Perpetua I'm afraid of the fire, I'm afraid, I am so
Afraid of fire.

The voice of Reddleman is heard outside the door

Reddleman (*off*)Your Grace! All right, all right, your Grace!

Duke The voice of tomorrow morning, after all.
The kind world intervenes.

Reddleman enters

Reddleman Ah, you poor sinners. I'm with you now;
Did you think I was never coming?

Perpetua   Never coming,
Never, never coming!

Duke How do you propose to rescue us, Reddleman?
And how the hell did you get here?

Reddleman   By me flair
For elementary science. I thumbed a lift
On the rising heat. I've got me nerve again;
For there's the conflagration below, frumping
And grouching like all the golden lads of lions
I ever put me hand into the fire of!
Didn't God make sinners of you and trap you here
For the decent purpose of putting me back
In the way of salvation?

Duke   And us, too, I hope.
Can we go the way you came?

Perpetua   God be kind,
Be kind.

Reddleman Have you any objection, now,
To dropping from time to time into me arms
From a great way off? T'would be to avoid the stairs,
Themselves being gone entirely.

Perpetua Must it be that way?

Reddleman   In the Captain's keeping,
Via Leo, con brio, the way of the lions!

Duke He's got himself well up in the god class now,
Perpetua: all we have to do is trust ourselves
To the rope of his nerve, spit on our hands, and go.

Bates appears at the window

Act II, Scene 1

Bates Well, *you've* got yourselves in a picklin' walls-up
And no mistake.

Duke   Are we to have all
The guardian angels at a blow?
You spoil us, Bates.

Reddleman   He spoils me night of glory.
Send him about his business, if you love me,
Your Grace, for the love of God, send him
About his business!

Bates   Couldn't the Lord Lieutenant
Even keep his nose out of this little job?
Come on, miss; come and take a butcher's
At the panorama; it's lovely outside 'ere.

Duke How do you think we're going to get down, Bates?

Bates Well, I come up by the ladders, but according
To the rules we have to slip down by the snakes. Still,
Do what your fancy tells you, mate. I'm
Not looking.

Perpetua   And I wish I hadn't looked, and I wish
We were safe on the ground.

Duke   Think of something high
Like Kanchenjunga. That very nearly takes us
Down the ladder before we start.

Reddleman   Your Grace,
You're not so out of your mind as to go
Out of the window? Encouraging robbery
And violence, you are, to set your foot
On a ladder propped up against your property
Without permission.

Duke Reddleman, by all means love your lions,
But condescend to the snakes. Come on.

Perpetua leaves by the window

Bates Let me take you, miss; fink nuffing of it.
Relax yourself, as though you was mink.
Fink lovely foughts, miss, and you won't weigh nuffing.
Wonder what stretch I'll have to do for abduction?

Duke (*climbing through the window after them*) A beautiful room,
   Reddleman; worth a fortune
In memories and astronomical equipment.

   The Duke disappears from view

Reddleman leans out

Reddleman H'wot do you think the dear God gave me back
   Me nerve for? To come crawling after heathen
   Like spittle down to a window? B'Jason,
   I've a better opinion of meself.

He crosses the room, throws open the door, and meets the glare of the fire

   Tossing your mighty manes, roaring yellow murder!
   The Captain's not afraid!

   Reddleman exits

*The Duke climbs back in at the window calling Reddleman. He races across
the room to the door*

Duke (*calling*) Reddleman, you hell-raking maniac!
   (*He picks up the half-eaten apple from the dressing table; calling to
   Reddleman*)
   Who would have the heart to disappoint you?

   *He puts the apple between his teeth and follows Reddleman the way of the
   stairs*

CURTAIN

SCENE 2

The Temple of the Ancient Virtues. An hour or so later

The light from the burning house is reflected in the lake

Rosabel is sobbing in the dark

*Dominic enters carrying two chairs and a stable lantern. He halts and listens to
the sobbing*

Dominic May I interrupt your unhappiness,
   Just to bring in one or two things? It's begun

To rain. Everything's going to get wet.
I wonder if you need cry quite so despairingly.
It makes me feel very awkward. I am not good
At comforting people, even when I know
Where to look for them. I'm Dominic Reedbeck ...
How do you do? And where would you be?

Rosabel   Oh, no,
Don't look for me.

Dominic   I couldn't look for you;
I don't know who you are. Everyone
Is safe, you know; they're all accounted for,
Except Miss Fleming. Do you know where she is?

Rosabel No. No, I don't know where she is.
Or where she ever will be now.
It would be better if no-one saw her again.

Dominic Why? Is she so badly burnt? Oh, what is it,
What *is* it? I wish you'd help me to be helpful;
I find it so difficult.

Rosabel   I'm over here.
I wish I were dead.

Dominic   I don't know how you can wish
For something you don't know anything about.
Now that it's started to rain you won't be the only one
Coming to shelter here. You should try
To pull yourself together. If I were you.

Rosabel Nobody will come to look for me in hell.
That's where I am.

Dominic   Oh yes, they will do.
It's the obvious place to look for anybody
It seems to me.

Rosabel   Well, thank you at any rate
For the chill in your voice. It's what I need:
Contempt enough to feel judgement's being done:
Then I may get back to a kind of reality,
Horrible though it will be,
Instead of being locked up in a nightmare ...
It was I who started the fire. I did it deliberately.

Dominic Perpetua was there. The Duke was there.
They might never have got away.

Rosabel But you haven't understood. You can't
Have understood. It was I—I—*I*
Who did this unimaginable thing.

Dominic I was thinking of myself.
My sister was there because I sent her there.
Perhaps you were chosen to be the instrument
By which I was shown the error I had fallen into.
If so, then I must thank you. Thank you, Miss Fleming.

Rosabel I don't know what you mean. You don't suppose
I've driven myself right out of the decent world
For your sake? Why won't you understand me?

Dominic I do understand. I know only too well
Our preternatural aptitude for sin.
My father made it quite clear to me.

Rosabel Where can I go away from myself?

Dominic   There's Sergeant
Harry Bullen, the policeman from Swinford Magna.
He's a very reasonable chap.
I'm sure he'd arrest you willingly if you asked him.
And he's here already, which is very convenient for you.

Rosabel Yes, where? Where is he?

Dominic I saw him, not so many minutes ago,
Coming head first down a ladder, to show the Duke
(As he said) that in the ordinary course of living
It makes little difference which way up you are.
He was joking, I think.

Rosabel   Joking? That seems so strange;
That someone can still be joking, in this place
Where I made it all happen. I'll go and find him
And give myself up. That's a joke, too—
I had given myself up as a hopeless case already.
What am I looking like? Well, it can hardly matter,
Though I don't want to look like a crazy woman
Even if I have become one. How gruesome it is—
To find that I am a dangerous eccentric
Unfit for society.
I was a better thing once.

Now I shall give myself up.
But please God help me to avoid the Duke
Wherever he may be.

The Duke enters, carrying things salvaged from the fire and over his shoulders a string of Chinese lanterns

Duke   He's down at the Temple,
I think, putting up some lanterns which he found
In a box. You'll find him there, presumably
Intent on some small ceremony of his own.
Though fairly uncertain whether it's obsequies
Or jubilation; he's in two hearts about it.
And both weigh heavier than the one he had.
God bless you, Rosabel; hold these; for a time
We thought we had lost you.

Rosabel   Did you think so? Lost me?

Dominic You must tell him now. It will be much easier now;
No postponing.

Dominic exits

Duke It's important that we should offset the smacking of the furies
With a little decorous gaiety, with a show
Of holier, if also homelier, flames.
The lanterns, Rosabel. They'll be very pale
Compared with the foment of wild flamboyant rose
We have in the sky to-night; but never mind;
Think what deeds of spring are done
By the glow-worm light of a primrose.

Rosabel I started the fire.

Duke   How did you come to do that?
A careless flash from your incendiary eyes,
Perhaps.

Rosabel God help me, it's the fearful miserable truth I'm telling you.
You won't want to believe it, but you have to.
I set fire to the wing. Of course nothing
Can be an explanation—no, not even
A deep-rooted unhappiness turned suddenly savage.
I destroyed the observatory
To bring you down to be among the rest of us,
To make you see what's going on below you.
But I know there's no way of redeeming what I did.

I'm destroyed along with the rest. But, oh, my dear,
You must be sure of one thing; I didn't know
That you were there, I didn't know
That any living soul was there!

Duke   O,
O, O, O, Rosabel:
If you had only asked me first.
I could have told you no fire would be enough
To burn down heaven, and while it's there
I shall find some wide-eyed place where I can sit
And scrutinize the inscrutable, amazed
That we can live in such a condition of mystery
And not be exasperated out of our flesh.
As we might be, were it not that flesh
Is interesting, too.
Your fire was too small, Rosabel, though enough
To singe my butler into ecstacy,
And smoke tears into eyes unaccustomed to them,
Mine, I mean. So much I delighted in
Is now all of ash, like a dove's breast feathers
Drifting dismally about the garden.

Rosabel Time and I both know how to bring
Good things to a sorry end, all in the course of love.
I know my grief can't hope to comfort you.
Tonight will go past, the horror of it, and the scars,
And the rest of life will go past, lamed, but it will go.
But I can never return what I have lost you
Or lose the evil that I made
Though the long steadiness of time
May long to make us well.

Duke So much I delighted in is all of ash.

Rosabel, giving a moan almost too low to hear, exits

Perpetua enters and takes Rosabel's place

The Duke, now hanging the lanterns, hasn't seen the change

But the lost world of walls and stairs,
Where I could cosset ghosts for their melancholy
Charm, has let the daylight into me
With a straight left of love. So no remorse,
Rosabel. I love my love, and my love loves me.
Everything goes but everything comes.
We fall away into a future, and all

The seven seas, and the milky way
And morning, and evening, and hi-cockalorum are in it.
Nothing is with the past except the past.
So you can make merry with the world, Rosabel
My grateful thanks.

Perpetua I have to make you understand.

Duke   I forgive you:
You can mine the lake so that it bursts
In a hundred and one torrential rainbows
Over the roof of the Carpenters' Arms; you can shatter
Conservatories into a deluge of crystal,
And shoot the cowman's nine insufferable
Children: I forgive you in advance.
I've achieved the rare, benevolent place
Where the irk of the lonely human state
Is quite unknown, and the fumbling fury
We call our life—It wasn't Rosabel
Who spoke then. It was surely Perpetua?

Perpetua I have to make you understand. You must
Be patient with me.

Duke   God so, it's the little firebird.
Are you rested? Lanterns, you see, to light our love.
I thought we could sit by the cinders
And toast our hearts, if Bates, as he was told to,
Brings the champagne.

Perpetua   You have to give me
Your best and gentlest attention. Be
At your most understanding. I need it, if I don't
Deserve it from you. To-night, when we seemed
Closely, and only us of all the living
World, attended by a dragon breathing out
Almost certain death——

*Bates enters with champagne and glasses in a bucket, and carrying another
lantern*

Bates   That Captain Reddleman,
As he likes to demean hisself to call hisself—
Now you're not getting yourselves into anuvver
Critical situation? You can scramble down
Off of that one on your own
Virgin initiative; I'm badgered if I'm going
To throw anuvver expensive rescue party.

Duke Matches, Perpetua?

Perpetua   No.

Bates   His illuminated
Lordship Reddleman should ought to have
His brain looked into. In and out, in and out,
In and out of the burning building, like
A perishing nigger in and out of a flaming
Woodpile. And what he says about me's
Enough to arrest a cock in the middle of his crow
And bring a blush to his ruddy comb. It isn't
The language I've been brought up to.

Duke (*lighting the lanterns*)   The first astonishment
Of creation; after that came the frenzy.

Perpetua   Let me
Talk to you.

Bates   Here's his incandescent majesty
Coming now, wiv his head under the table.

Reddleman enters, carrying a table on his head

What's the matter, mate; lost your tit-fer?

Reddleman There's no doubt at all Your Grace has noticed
There are some men are born too small in the soul
To do gratifying deeds, and not sprain all decency.
And 'tis the footman Bates
Who's the diminuendo of all small souls.
He's a demi-semi soul, and that's magnanimous.
I have to put on me glasses, and then search
As if 'twas how I was looking for a louse
In Molly O'Magan's obster-eperous hair.
Would it be here you were wanting the table set up,
Your Grace?

Duke   Put it where the wind won't blow;
It's blowing cold. And for Christmas' sake
Will you pair of immortals kiss each other
And come off the tiles?

Bates I'd just like to know who give him permission
To go measuring my soul? I never done.
I've got it nicely laid away: spotless,
Wiv lavender.

Reddleman   'Twas a mighty night of miracle,
With Cuchulain at me right hand, and Daniel at me left,
And the smallest soul in the world dashes it from me,
And he naked in his shirt.

Duke   Ah, miracles, Reddleman,
Miracles; don't trust them. How far
Can a man journey on a miracle? It's better
To bounce your behind on any spavined hack
Than to straddle a flash of lightning.
Straighten your laurel wreaths, the couple of you,
And remember one another in your prayers.
It seems I have something else to listen to.

Reedbeck and Dominic enter

Reedbeck Ah, here he is. I'm not what you thought me, your Grace.
I must tell you plainly I'm not at all what you thought me.

Duke No?

Reedbeck No. If you ask these men to go, your Grace,
I shall be only too grieved to tell you what I am.

Bates (*to Reddleman*) Nuffing to stay for, boy. I'll come and see you
Popping yourself in and out of the fire again.

Reddleman Breakfast, your Grace, at what o'clock?

Duke   The morning
Must wait, Reddleman. I have still
The rest of the night to consider.

Bates and Reddleman exit

Perpetua (*to Reedbeck*)   Darling,
Not now. Any day or night of the year,
There's always time, you can go together, and look
At the pigs or the winter wheat, and talk your two
Hearts out; but just this night, and for just
These five minutes of this night, leave me
To talk to him alone.

Reedbeck   I've worked myself up,
I've reached the pitch now; it would never do
To put it—put it off; walked much too fast,
Breath very short, and then heart very heavy,
Imagination—disconcerting—too vivid: I see you

Both up there, no amount of stars
Any use, in dreadful danger, and who but me,
I, whichever it is, responsible?

Dominic Please blame me for that. Do allow me
To know which sin belongs to whom. We shall only
Get confused, Father, unless you keep strictly
To your own wrong turning.

Reedbeck   Extremely difficult
To know where to stop, once you begin to believe
You're not all you should be. Let me see,
There was something worse Dominic said
I had to confess to you.

Perpetua   He knows, he knows.
So now, you poor worried Poppadillo, half
Awash with sleep, you can go back
To bed at once, or else I think I shall cry.

Reedbeck But I don't quite know what you know he knows,
And I think I'd better—

Duke   Drink, Reedbeck, I think
You'd better drink. We have something to celebrate,
You and I, which lights me more than the most
Tower-toppling blaze that ever lit
A city lane—

Perpetua   Oh, do let me speak to you!

Reedbeck I've reached the pitch. I've worked myself up
To the point of whatever the point was when I first
Came in. But you're quite right, half awash, suddenly
Woken up in alarm—

Dominic   Now, *think* a minute.

Duke Master Dominic: pass to your saintly father
This glass of champagne.

Reedbeck   Excuse me. But I know
There's some good reason why I shall have to refuse.
Now that my attention has been drawn
To what must be a myopia in my moral vision—
Must have been suffering from it all my life,
I suppose: and tonight feels very latter-day;
Wrath of God: here we are

Looking such weak vessels and so temporary
Among the four terrible elements
(The rain and the fireman's hose remind me of the fourth)—
What was I going to say? Yes, yes, I think
It wouldn't be correct to drink with you before
I give myself up to Sergeant Bullen.

Duke   Drink up,
And keep your sins for some leisurely angel;
They've nothing to do with me. Dominic,
If what appear to be discrepancies
In your father's books afflict you, let me tell you
Though they seem unusual they're as much in order
As Sergeant Bullen's collar and tie. There exists
A document assigning to your father
All those percentages from rents and sales
Which you seem to have thought are misbegotten.

Dominic Do you mean you've noticed the discrepancies
And legalized them?

Duke   My dear conscience-nudging,
Parent-pesting, guilt-corroded child,
If I may address you with so much affection,
The arrangement was perfect. It embarrassed
Neither of us. Take a drink to wash
Your conscience down. And one brimming for you,
Perpetua.

Perpetua It's too full, seriously,
Far too full. You've been good to my father.
Please will you put it down? I know my hand
Isn't steady enough to take it.

Duke   Then let me sip
Some away from the western rim
And leave the east for you.

Reedbeck   Made it legal?

Duke There now. Shall we drink
To the babe born in the fire, the crowning of souls
In extremity? As long as we live, Perpetua,
We shall be able to tell how, at midnight,
We skated over death's high-lit ebony
And heard the dark ring a change of light,
While everywhere else the clocks
Were sounding the depths of a dark, unhappy end.

And then we shall be able to say
How an autumn duke—

Perpetua   —found that fear could seem
Like love to a silly girl, who now knows
It was fear and not love, wishes you to forgive her,
Wishes she could sink away with the night
Where she won't any more trouble you.

Duke (*after a long pause, raising his glass*) Then the toast is: Fear.

Perpetua I had to tell you.

Duke   Do I
Have to drink alone?

Perpetua   No. No.

They all drink in silence

Duke Do you think I can't forgive you? I forgive
Both of us for being born of the flesh,
Which means I forgive all tossing and turning,
All foundering, all not finding,
All irreconcilability,
All the friction of this great orphanage
Where no one knows his origin and no one
Comes to claim him. I forgive even
The unrevealing revelation of love
That lifts a lid purely
To close it, and leaves us knowing that greater things
Are close, but not to be disclosed
Though we die for them. I forgive
Everything, my most dear Perpetua
Except that I wasn't born something less ambitious,
Such as a Muscovy duck.

Reedbeck   I couldn't think
Of allowing such generosity. Legalized!
No, your Grace, I simply couldn't accept it.

Duke Reedbeck, my God! For how many years have you
Stood here? You must be very old by now.
I remember you well in happier times.

Perpetua   Poppadillo,
Why do we all have to get between someone else
And the sun? Keep me from doing this again.

Reedbeck Whatever you say, my dear; though whatever you're saying
  I really don't know. I'd like to help, but you're both
  Talking in my sleep, evidently.

  Edgar, Jessie and Hilda enter

Edgar That was a hideous mile or two of driving!
  We saw the fire on the clouds, and guessed
  It could only be here.

Hilda   I saw it from home, reflected
  In my bedroom window. I tried to telephone
  But I couldn't get through.

Duke   I must ask you, if you will,
  To remember we've been appreciating this very
  Minor act of God for more than two hours.
  The earth has moved on roughly a hundred
  And thirty thousand miles since then,
  And histories have been much altered.
  I hope the dance was a great success.

Jessie   Yes, lovely,
  But it's doing myself a great kindness to be able
  To sit down. Dancing all hours, and a couple of miles
  Of apprehension makes All Hallowe'en
  Into a marathon if a girl's not quite
  As hale and hallow as once she was.
  Is everybody safe?

Duke   Safe: I'll not say
  "As houses", considering what goes on,
  But as safe and suffering as health can be.

Hilda It's a fortunate thing that providence
  Was in her friendly mood to-night
  And kept you out of Galileo's lap.

Duke Not she. She saw two souls there, happily occupied
  At the narrow end of the telescope,
  Two star-loving minutiae, male and female,
  Perpetua and my unoffending self:
  And instantly shot out a vituperative
  Tongue. And we were rescued by two
  Heavenly agents, Bates and Reddleman.

Reedbeck God bless them; I've never liked either of them,
  But God bless them.

Hilda   And keep them in the heavenly business.

Jessie I'll kiss them for it presently. They must
Have got a bit above themselves
To rescue you from there.

Edgar   And so
You meant to meet there, even this afternoon.
And the only comfort I had, all the way home,
Was that Perpetua was safely sleeping
Away in another house.

Perpetua   We meant to meet there,
And this afternoon we were lying to you,
And never was a lie less happy for everyone.

Duke I hear me whistling down the wind.

Jessie   We wouldn't
Like you to think we're setting up in competition,
But in our own small way we've met
With a catastrophe, too.

Hilda   Both our cars
Swung in at the gates together, and as our attention
Was all on the fire—

Jessie   Our wings aren't what they were,
As Lucifer said after his long day's fall.

Duke What's the matter with the Fates to-day; fidget, fidget;
Why can't they settle down to some useful spinning?
I forgot to ask you, Hilda (Jessie and Lucifer
Remind me), how is Roderic?

Hilda   Asleep when I left.
Two ribs broken, and a slight concussion,
No worse than that. But that was quite enough
To tell me how intolerable it would be
To see him badly disabled, or perhaps dying.
I found myself sitting beside him marvelling
At the thought of all the human lives
Which had crossed the centuries to bring him about,
And however much he may try to be the same
As everybody else, how can he be?
He is Roderic-the-only-once, Roderic
Phenomenon, and now Roderic in pain
This afternoon I made a cockshy of him—

But this afternoon I was as poor-sighted
As I was accusing him of being, poor darling.
I must get back home. I only wanted to be
Quite certain no one was hurt.

Duke   Rosabel
Is hurt.

Edgar   But we saw her with Harry Bullen;
She seemed most vigorous, talking his helmet off;
He was mopping his head with a handkerchief.

Duke   Rosabel
Why? With Harry Bullen? Why should she be?

Dominic Because she thought it was necessary
To her peace of mind. She has given herself up.

Duke And I give you up! How, by hell's grand canyon,
Do you know she has?

Dominic   She was really very unhappy;
I think I helped her to decide.

Jessie   But why?
Given herself up for lost, or what?

Duke   You strapping,
Ice-cold, donkey-witted douche of tasteless water!
I could willingly—Dominic, dear boy,
God would tell me He loves you, but then God
Is wonderfully accomplished, and to me
You seem less lovely, and for this good reason:
You think more of the sin than of the sinner.
Poor Rosabel. Where shall we find her?

Hilda   When
We saw them they were standing by the sundial.
What has she done?

Duke   Loved me beyond her strength.
We go and get her out of the arms of the law,
However attractive Bullen's arms may be.
Dear Rosabel! And after that we must find
Beds for ourselves away from the smell of smouldering
Memory. Bring along some of the lanterns.
Excellent, blessed Rosabel. Ros-a-bel!

The Duke goes, calling her. Hilda follows him

Reedbeck (*to Jessie*) Beds, yes, yes, beds, quite important.
There's one at least at my house if you'd care to oblige it,
Care to make use of it. No more sleep for me
To-night; it wouldn't be wise; I've only just
Managed to digest the sleep I've had already.
In something of a fuddle.

Jessie   Dear, I'd get
Into anybody's bed to-night, and sleep
Without a murmur, even in the arms of Morpheus
If he'd give up his lute and let me. Where's the step?

Jessie goes out, Reedbeck holding a lantern for her, as he follows her

Dominic A fine rain raining still. Aren't you coming, Perpetua?

Perpetua I'll stay in the dry and rest.

Dominic I was hoping to talk to you, to tell you, to say
How responsible I feel for all that fear
And danger, I mean yours to-night. I expect
You think I was very much to blame.

Perpetua   No,
Dominic.

Dominic   They think I'm altogether wrong,
All the time. But I don't know how that can be.
And yet the whole of life is so unconsidering,
Bird, beast, and fish, and everything,
I wonder how the Creator came to be
Mixed up in such company. Do you think I'm wrong?

Perpetua No, Dominic.

Dominic (*with a sigh*)   Ethics are very difficult.

Dominic goes into the rain

Perpetua and Edgar are left. They sit in silence for a moment

Edgar Did you forget I was here?

Perpetua   I didn't forget.
But I wish I could forget, and I wish you had forgotten,
This afternoon's brazen lying.

Edgar   I have forgotten.
Why should we remember this afternoon
When probably no one else does?

Perpetua   But am I sure
I want you to forget as incuriously as that?
I want your father not to be hurt by to-night,
I want you not to be hurt by this afternoon,
I want to be free to make my own way,
But I want to be remembered.

Edgar   My memory
Is for nothing else. But, as it happens,
I hardly need it. Over and over again
I see you for the first time. I round
Some corner of my senses, and there, as though
The air had formed you out of a sudden thought,
I discover you. Any memory I had
Vanishes, to let you in so unannounced
My whole body stammers with surprise.
I imagine I love you. And I don't think
You can fairly object, when all you have to do
Is walk freely through my thoughts and round
My heart. You needn't even turn your head.

Perpetua Don't say this now. I'm still remembering
I can give pain, and that in itself is loss
Of liberty.

Edgar   No, I just mentioned it in passing.

Perpetua No one is separate from another; how difficult
That is. I move, and the movement goes from life
To life all round me. And yet I have to be
Myself. And what is *my* freedom becomes
Another person's compulsion. What are we to make
Of this dilemma?

Edgar   I haven't the sense to ask.
Whatever the human mystery may be
I am it.

Perpetua There's comfort in that.

Edgar   Tell me:
Do I seem to you to be only a sort
Of postscript to my father?

Perpetua   No Edgar.
Across and across my heart, never at all.

Edgar I begin to notice myself, too,
I must say. Here the little parents come.

The Duke and Reedbeck enter

So now the house goes with a dragging wing.
Are your spirits very heavy, Father?

Duke   They ride;
No, no, they ride well enough.

Reedbeck (*to Perpetua*)   Isn't it time
My all night wanderer went to bed?

Duke   She will stay
For a moment's peaceful conversation.

Perpetua I want to know about Rosabel. When Dominic said—

Duke I'll keep her story for a rainy day.

Edgar And for now the rain has blown over. Shall we go
And see how the last of the flames dance down
To sleep among the ruins, Perpetua?

Duke Our peaceful conversation, Perpetua.

Edgar Perpetua?

Perpetua   I'll find my way to bed.

Edgar I shall take the liberty to light you there.
Tomorrow, then, Father.

Duke   Tomorrow to you.

Perpetua Tomorrow to us all, but not too soon.
I need the soft pillows to make my peace
Before I trust myself to another day tomorrow.

Edgar and Perpetua exit

Reedbeck is almost asleep in a chair

Duke Shall I be sorry for myself? In mortality's name

I'll be sorry for myself. Branches and boughs
Brown hills, the valleys faint with brume,
A burnish on the lake; mile by mile
It's all a unison of ageing,
The landscape's all in tune, in a falling cadence,
All decaying. And nowhere does it have to hear
The quips of spring, or, when so nearing its end,
Have to bear the merry mirth of May.
How fortunate to grow in the crow-footed woods,
Eh, Reedbeck? But I see you're anxious to sleep.

Reedbeck I? No, no; I'll never go to sleep
Again to-night, much too disturbed.
Don't know what to suggest I make of anything.
I only hope a quiet dignity
Will meet the case. Civilization is simply
(If I had to define it) simply dignity,
Simply simple dignity; but then
Sons and daughters come into it, most lovable,
Most difficult, and unexpected combustion,
And so forth and so forth. Now le Roi Soleil,
How many children did he have? One legitimate,
Several illegitimate ... le Duc de Maine,
La Duchesse de Chartres ...

Duke   Shall I be happy for myself?
In the name of existence I'll be happy for myself.
Why, Reedbeck, how marvellous it is to moulder.
Think how you would have felt when you were lying
Grubbing in your mother's womb,
With only a wall to look at,
If you could have seen in your embryonic eye
The realm of bryony, sloes, rose-hips,
And a hedge's ruin,
A countryside like a drowned angel
Lying in shallow water, every thorn
Tendering a tear. Think, Reedbeck,
Think of the wonder of such glimmering woe;
How in a field of milk-white haze the lost
Apollo glows and wanders towards noon;
The wind-blown webs are brighter,
The rolling apples warmer than the sun.
Heavens! you would have cried, the womb
Echoing round you: These are the heavens, and I,
Reedbeck, am stillborn. Would you not?

Reedbeck (*waking slightly*) And la Duchesse de Condè, I think.

Duke So with ourselves; imagine: to have the sensation
    Of nearness of sight, shortness of breath,
    Palpitation, creaking in the joints,
    Shootings, stabbings, lynching of the limbs,
    A sudden illumination of lumbago.
    What a rich world of sensation to achieve,
    What infinite variety of being.
    Is it not?

Reedbeck Dominic not fond ...
    Perpetua ...

Duke   Reedbeck, I have to tell you
    I mean to marry. I can still remember,
    In my ebbing way, how pleasant it is to love;
    An ancient love can blow again, like summer
    Visiting St Martin. A breath will do it.
    If the breath comes deep, and deep it has come.
    You must give me your felicitations. I marry
    Rosabel, when Rosabel
    (After six months, I understand)
    Is disengaged from custody.

Only deep breathing comes from Reedbeck

    Thank you, dear fellow. Rosabel
    Would thank you, too, if she were here.
    She and I, sharing two solitudes,
    Will bear our spirits up to where not even
    The nightingale can know,
    Where the song is quiet, and quiet
    Is the song. Tell me, Reedbeck, before
    We leave each other in sleep, where would you say
    The lonely moment is coaxing us to go?

Reedbeck gives a gentle near-whistling snore

    Well, yes, yes, quite so, my little one,
    It comes to that in the end.

CURTAIN

FURNITURE AND PROPERTY LIST

Only essential properties, furniture, etc are listed here, as mentioned in the text. Further dressing can be added at the director's discretion

ACT I

SCENE 1

On stage: Day bed
Table. *On it:* telephone, bowl of apples, pairs of dark glasses
Mirror

Off stage: Telegram on salver **(Reddleman)**

Personal: **Reedbeck:** wristwatch, shilling
Perpetua: Bag, holster with small, loaded revolver

SCENE 2

Strike: Previous set

Set: Exterior, Temple of Ancient Virtues

Off stage: Writing case and pen **(Jessie)**
Bow and quiver of arrows **(Duke)**
Bow and quiver of arrows **(Edgar)**

ACT II

SCENE 1

Strike: Previous set

Set: As for Act I, SCENE 1
Oil lamp on table

SCENE 2

Strike: Previous set

Set: As for Act I, SCENE 2

Off stage: Lantern **(Dominic)**
Two chairs **(Dominic)**
Four Chinese lanterns **(Duke)**
Salvage from fire **(Duke)**
Bucket with bottle of champagne and glasses **(Bates)**
Lantern **(Bates)**
Table **(Reddleman)**
Box of matches **(Bates)**

LIGHTING PLOT

One interior setting, one exterior setting. Practical fittings required:
1 oil lamp, 2 lanterns, 4 Chinese lanterns

ACT I, SCENE 1

To open: Interior. Autumn morning
No cues

ACT I, SCENE 2

To open: Exterior lighting. Autumn afternoon. Light reflected from lake
No cues

ACT II, SCENE 1

To open: Interior. Night (darkness)

Cue 1	**Perpetua** enters *Light overspills from corridor. Cut when Perpetua closes door*	(Page 47)
Cue 2	**Duke** lights oil lamp *Snap on covering spot*	(Page 48)
Cue 3	**Duke** opens door *Fire effect below*	(Page 56)
Cue 4	**Reddleman** throws open the door *Fire effect*	(Page 60)

ACT II, SCENE 2

To open: Exterior. Night. Light reflected from lake

Cue 5	**Duke** lights lanterns *Snap on covering spots*	(Page 66)

EFFECTS PLOT

Act I

Cue 1   **Duke:** "Filled for your next big scene."   (Page 26)
         Dinner gong

ACT II

Cue 2   **Duke** opens door   (Page 56)
         Fire roar

Cue 3   **Reddleman** throws open the door   (Page 60)
         Fire roar

Cue 4   To open Scene 2   (Page 60)
         Gentle rain. Continue throughout scene

MADE AND PRINTED IN GREAT BRITAIN BY
LATIMER TREND & COMPANY LTD PLYMOUTH

MADE IN ENGLAND